The day before their mission, 13 out of the 25 planes sent out by the 445th Bomb Group did not return from combat to their base at Tibenham, England. That was 130 men, ten men per bomber, who did not return to their home base. They were either wounded, killed, taken prisoner, or had to evade capture. Many of them never returned home from the war. It meant that dozens of men would never live to marry, have families, or see their loved ones again. It was one of the worst losses in U.S. 8th Air Force history by a heavy bomber group up to that point. The chances of survival of a 30-mission tour of duty for a ten-man bomber crew were less than twenty-five percent. This is the story of one of the crews under Jimmy Stewart's command, the Williams crew, and one of their most dangerous missions when they flew deeper into a heavily-defended Germany than any previous mission. Flying in the lead plane in their formation was none other than Major James "Jimmy" M. Stewart, the famous movie actor-turned-bomber pilot, their squadron commander. This is the detailed account of that mission and the incredible story of one of their squadron's most uniquely named planes and other brave crews who flew it in WWII, including Fox News anchor Eric Shawn's father, Gilbert Shawn. The plane and its crews still have a message for us today.

"FOR HE SHALL GIVE HIS ANGELS CHARGE OVER THEE TO KEEP THEE IN ALL THY WAYS"

Biblical quote from Psalm 91:11 engraved on
Brigadier General James "Jimmy" M. Stewart's grave marker

"I am not overly religious, but learned to be sincerely religious at 20,000 ft. in the air.
I could recite the 91st Psalm to myself [on] many missions. I could relate it to our situation.
[*Speaking of the Williams crew*]… we had probably the best B-24 crew in Europe"

The Williams crew radio operator T/Sgt. Frank Mangan in a letter to a
fellow 703rd Bomb Squadron member, Harold "Robbie" Robinson, in 1989

"Thank God for a 10-man crew!"

1st Lt. William "Mack" M. Williams
From his notes in the debriefing report for the
February 25, 1944 mission to Nurnberg, Germany

THE U.S. EIGHTH AIR FORCE IN WORLD WAR II

The Mighty Eighth compiled an impressive record in the war. This achievement, however, carried a high price. Half of the U.S. Army Air Force's casualties in WW II were suffered by the Eighth Air Force (more than 47,000 casualties, with more than 26,000 dead*). Seventeen Medals of Honor went to Eighth Air Force personnel during the war. By war's end, they had been awarded a number of other medals to include 220 Distinguished Service Crosses, and 442,000 Air Medals. Many more awards were made to Eighth Air Force veterans after the war that remain uncounted. There were 261 fighter aces in the Eighth Air Force during World War II. Thirty-one of these aces had 15 or more aircraft kills apiece. Another 305 enlisted gunners were also recognized as aces.

*This was more than the U.S. Marines lost in all of WWII.

FACT SHEET

UNITED STATES AIR FORCE

http://www.8af.af.mil/library/factsheets/factsheet_print.asp?fsID=17064&page=1

REVIEWS

"This book is an excellent account and record of Capt. William "Mack" Williams crew, and how they responded to an emergency on their mission #13 and managed to land the "Nine Yanks and a Jerk" safely. Just one of 29 mission's they walked away from." WWII veteran, T/Sgt. George Snook, flight engineer and top turret gunner on the Williams crew who flew on *Nine Yanks and a Jerk* as described in the book. 703rd Bomb Squadron, 445th Bomb Group, Ohio

"Scott Culver describes the WWII experiences of his father's B-24 crew in this well researched and finely detailed record of their journey from training to combat, highlighting their most dangerous mission on which they narrowly survived an 88mm shell blast through their aircraft as they penetrated deep into Germany. It's a compelling read for any WWII aviation buff." Col. Doug Hillstrom, USAF (Ret.), Colorado

"The author has done his research. This is a compelling history of a B-24 Liberator that saw extensive combat in Europe, the crews that flew that ship and the eventual crash of that ship in a field in Belgium... and, the heroism of the Belgium Resistance who rescued some of the crew from the crash... This book should be a must read for anyone who wants to know the sacrifices these young men made for love of country and freedom from tyranny." Rob Metcalf, nephew of Earle Metcalf (the pilot of the crew who originally named and flew *Nine Yanks and a Jerk*), Wisconsin

"I was there. Very authentic. Read it all in two days. Couldn't put it down." WWII veteran, M/Sgt. Paul "Rusty" Rostock. 702nd Bomb Squadron, 445th Bomb Group, Idaho

"Well-researched and full of photos making this an excellent research and nostalgia book, especially for family members of those who fought in World War II and more particularly in B-24s." Charlie Doggett, nephew of Earl Doggett (engineer/gunner on the original crew that named and flew the legendary plane), Costa Rica

"This book is the result of an extraordinary process initiated by Scott and that caused him to travel many countries. Scott makes [it clear] through this book [it is] a real tribute to his father. The book allows you to follow this approach and to immerse yourself 70 years back." Benjamin Heylen, museum curator of *Musee du Souvenir 40-45*, Maleves, Belgium

"After getting my own copy, I bought several more to give to all the aviation and history buffs I know. I especially bought one for my 98 year-old father-in-law who worked as an instructor at Consolidated where this B-24 was built." Penny, California

"A wonderful book put together by a son's passion and dedication of his father's WW2 exploits, telling not only his father's memories but with meticulous research the book tells the tales of those men and women who served with the US 8th Army Air force while serving in the English country side of East Anglia, including famed Hollywood actor Jimmy Stewart. Nicely put together for anybody wanting a good read and a very useful publication for historians. The book concentrates on a B-24 Liberator heavy American bomber from the 445th Bomb Group based at Tibenham, Norfolk named Nine Yanks and a Jerk. Already looking forward to the next publication by this author." Andrew, England

See more reviews at WWW.SONOFAGUNNERB24.COM

U.S. Eighth Air Force

445th Bomb Group

703rd Bomb Squadron

NINE YANKS AND A JERK

The incredible saga of one of the most legendary planes in the U.S. 8th Air Force flown by Major James M. Stewart and the aircrews under his command in World War II.

True stories of courage while under fire, skillful leadership, and survival against all odds.

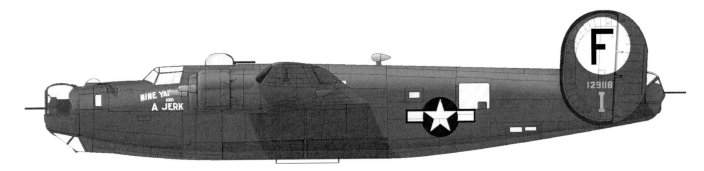

B-24H Liberator   Serial Number 41-29118

Manufactured by Consolidated/Forth Worth

Researched and Written

by

Scott E. Culver

Son of S/Sgt. Henry J. Culver, Sr. - Ball turret/waist gunner/assistant engineer
445th Bombardment Group (Heavy), 703rd Bomb Squadron
Under Squadron Commander Major James M. Stewart at Tibenham, England
2nd Combat Wing, 2nd Air Division, U.S. 8th Air Force
European Theater of Operations (ETO), World War II

© 2015-2016

MORE REVIEWS

"I was watching the news several months back and saw you interviewed on the news... Everything about your book I loved and wanted to read. To my surprise my daughter got me your book for Christmas. I started reading it that night and did not put it down until I was finished. I just wanted to take the time to say, WELL DONE. The best book I've read in a long time. After all the research, places you have been, and the people you've met the only words that come to mind is, "what a great adventure." Thank you for the book and keep up the great work." Marty, Alabama

"A fabulous dedication to the author's father and all those brave young men and women that gave so much for us to have today and tomorrow..." Suzie, England

"Outstanding ~ I read the book in two sittings; and it held my interest like several other WWII books I found intriguing, including "Double Cross" and "The Girls of Atomic City." The author's writing style captures the events in a way that makes the reader feel a part of the experience and personally acquainted with the brave young men who participated in the subject mission. In addition, I felt I followed the author on his journey and got to know the wonderful people he met and who helped him along the way. The pictures in the book are an added bonus!" Janice, New Jersey

"What do you get a father who has one of the most complete WW2 libraries? 9 Yanks and a Jerk! He lit up! Thank you all." Donna, Arizona

"A tale of two adventures, one high over Nazi Germany in WWII and the other moving across continents and countries as a loving son traces his father's footsteps. Not only are the adventures fascinating to read, but the author has included many side bars of information, such as the 445th Bomb Group Formation Chart, that add depth and clarity to the reader's overall understanding. I too have shared a copy with my grandson." U.S. Air Force veteran, Bill, Ohio

"Great writer. The author tells a great story of our flyers in WWII. Awesome pictures. Can't wait for your next book 'Daylight Raiders.'" U.S. Army and Navy veteran, William, New Jersey

"Not just an Ordinary Bomber Tale. This story soars above the rest. Outstanding Story. I have the privilege of knowing one of the flight crew members and can attest that this story is every bit fascinating as it is true. A well-researched book, the author takes the time to explore intricate details that many would overlook in a more generalized warbird escapade or Pointblank Directive telltale. This is a must-have for every fan of aviation in World War II!" WhitmerWW2

"This is a fantastic book. I could not put it down. An amazing true war story and obviously written by someone who has been so very dedicated to ensuring the facts are correct and by someone with a passion for history. We are looking forward to the author's additional writing, Daylight Raiders. Thank you, Scott Culver, for a wonderful book!" 'Laceycat,' New Jersey

"The author's extensive research and attention to detail made me feel as if I were on the mission his dad flew from England to Nuremburg, Germany. I look forward to his next book, "Daylight Raiders" to learn about the other missions his father flew under the command of James (Jimmy) M. Stewart during WWII." Alan, New Jersey

See more reviews at WWW.SONOFAGUNNERB24.COM

CONTENTS

World War II
70th Anniversary
Commemoration
★ 1945-2015 ★

The above lapel pin of an American eagle, known as the "Ruptured Duck," was issued to military men and women of the U.S. Armed Forces who served honorably and were discharged during or at the end of World War II. It also came in the form of a patch to be sewn over the right pocket of one's service uniform. It was given the nickname because the rendition of the eagle looked more like a pregnant duck to the bearer. The veterans were allowed to wear their uniforms for 30 days after being discharged (due to clothing rationing) until they could acquire sufficient civilian attire. The lapel pin was to be worn on the uniform during that month as a sign that they had honorably served, were discharged, and were not AWOL (Absence Without Leave). It thus became an iconic symbol for World War II veterans.

It's hard to believe it's been 70 years since those historic events. The war in Europe had ended on May 8, 1945, and was thus designated as VE Day (Victory in Europe). The war, however, still raged in the Pacific for several more months. Even though the Japanese eventually surrendered in mid-August of 1945 after the two atomic bombs were dropped on Hiroshima on August 6th and Nagasaki on the 9th, President Harry S. Truman designated September 2, 1945 as VJ Day (Victory over Japan). The formal Japanese surrender was signed aboard the U.S.S. Missouri, with General Douglas MacArthur presiding over the ceremony, thus officially ending the greatest war the world had ever seen and experienced.

On September 2, 2015, I traveled to Washington D.C. to the National World War II Memorial for the 70th Anniversary celebration of VJ Day. There were dozens of WWII veterans there, most of whom were in their late 80s and 90s. There were also hundreds of family members, the descendants of those brave men and women who fought for our freedoms and the liberation of Europe and the Pacific. There was also plenty of media as well. Many foreign dignitaries and representatives of the Allied nations who fought alongside us in the war were present. There were very memorable speeches and talks (including one from former senator and WWII veteran, 92 year old Bob Dole, whom I met there). In addition, the U.S. Navy's military band played several patriotic songs to accentuate the occasion. They looked brilliant in their dress white uniforms. It was very befitting that they played for the event, as the Navy and the Marines had played such a significant role to end the war in the Pacific. It was very well done and organized, in spite of the over 90 degree heat and high humidity.

One of the most memorable quotes I read along the granite panels at the memorial was that of President Truman. It speaks of those who fought in all theaters of the war - in the Pacific, North Africa, and in Europe. It reads as follows:

OUR DEBT TO THE HEROIC MEN AND VALIANT WOMEN IN THE SERVICE OF OUR COUNTRY CAN NEVER BE REPAID. THEY HAVE EARNED OUR UNDYING GRATITUDE. AMERICA WILL NEVER FORGET THEIR SACRIFICES.

President Truman's words ring true today as they did some 70 years ago. This is the legacy of my father and his generation. Their stories should never be forgotten, as theirs was the generation that fought and preserved our liberties in the greatest conflict in history. Every generation seems to have its tyrants and despots that have to be dealt with. Theirs had to deal with Germany's Hitler, Italy's Mussolini, and Japan's Hirohito. The pages contained within this work tell just a few of the innumerable stories of the brave airmen who served and fought in the European Theater of Operations, against Hitler. The dangers of aerial combat during the Strategic Bombing Campaign over northwest Europe are both legendary and horrific. Volumes of books, movies, and documentaries have been made about them, and rightly so. That is how we pass on to future generations some kind of appreciation for what these men and women did for our nation, and the world. We must never forget that freedom is never free. It comes at a high cost – the lives of Americans, and our allies. As I always told my students when I taught both American and World History courses, "Thank a veteran when you see one, because he or she risked his or her life for our freedoms." This holds true for our current military personnel as well. My prayer is that this work inspires us to remember how our freedoms have been preserved, and must continue to be. Lest we forget…

Scott Culver, 'Son of a Gunner' – Son of USAAF Staff Sergeant Henry J. Culver, Sr.
September 5, 2015

September 2, 2015 – VJ Day. Top: Me in front of the White House holding up an August 1945 replica newspaper announcing the end of the war. (I remember the date this way - VJ Day was September 2nd, my brother Hank Jr. was born on September 3rd, and my father was discharged on September 4th – all in 1945.) Below: Bob Dole and me (in my father's WWII uniform) at the World War II Memorial in Washington D.C. I thanked Mr. Dole for his WWII service, and told him about my father's WWII service and my book.

PREFACE

The mission date was February 25, 1944, the sixth and final mission of the Operation Argument raids. The raids, nicknamed 'Big Week,' were a series of intense week-long attacks on the German Luftwaffe and aviation industry. Soon after the 445th Bomb Group dropped their bombs on the aviation factory and airfield at Furth (near Nurnberg) Germany, enemy flak gunners continued tracking their formation. The 445th Bomb Group's formation of twelve planes was part of the 170 American B-24 heavy bombers that raided the German target. The accurate German anti-aircraft gunners were shooting .88mm shells that were exploding moderate to heavy bursts at the bombers' altitude at 18,000 feet. The exploding shells filled the sky all around the formation of B-24 Liberators with black puffs of smoke. Steel splinters from the exploding shells pierced their planes' thin-skinned hulls like a screwdriver through aluminum foil. The anxious crews could hear the steel splinters punch through the aluminum hull louder as each burst got closer. The smell of cordite from the bursts filled the air around the planes so intensely that the waist gunners could smell it through their oxygen masks at their open windows.

Right after bombs away, the formation had quickly dropped 500 feet in altitude from their 18,000 foot bombing altitude. ***Nine Yanks and a Jerk***, along with other B-24s from the 445th Bomb Group, descended and banked in a sharp left turn off the target to head back to the group's base in England. This was standard operating procedure, performed with the hopes of throwing off the German flak gunners' aim, and to allow the fleeing bombers to make a quicker escape from the target area. The air temperature outside was -30° F (-34° C). The two waist gunners in each plane felt it the most as they were standing at their gun positions in front of the open waist gun windows in their unpressurized aircraft. The slipstream and wind was over 160 miles per hour, just an arm's reach outside their windows. With that kind of wind and temperature, they had to fire their guns regularly to keep them from freezing up.

As the formation was making its turn, left waist gunner Staff Sergeant Hank Culver was firing his .50 caliber machine gun at several enemy planes near their formation. In spite of the deadly flak, the enemy's fighters were still within firing range of the heavy bomber formation. As the 160 pound, six foot tall, dark-haired and dark-eyed Culver fired at them, his machine gun was suddenly ripped from his hands by flying debris that came over the left wing from the front of the plane. Just a moment before, the crew felt a thud, which had caused the plane to shudder. They took a direct hit - an unexploded .88mm shell had pierced through their closed bomb bay doors!

The whizzing shell, which rattled the crew, tore out part of the bomb bay catwalk, missed the radio operator Technical Sergeant Frank Mangan by two feet, and also just missed the top turret gunner, Technical Sergeant George Snook. It immediately exited out the side of plane behind the pilot, 1st Lieutenant Mack Williams. The shell missed Williams by inches. The remains of the screeching shell had ricocheted off the armor plating fixed behind the pilot's seat, taking with it George Snook's packed parachute and unshod combat boots off the flight deck and sucked them out the hole. The exiting shell left a hole the size of a window on the side of the plane right behind the pilot. The wind howled through the new opening it created. The arctic air now pushed its way inside the plane right behind Mack's seat. The shell also ripped the pilot's half inch armor plating right off its moorings, which was only inches behind his position. As the flying debris was blown out of their new 'window' and passed over the left wing, it hit Culver's gun, tearing it out of his firmly gripped hands and knocked the gun sight off the end of his machine gun. Although the gun remained on its swivel post, the twenty year old gunner was startled and knocked off balance. He wondered what in the world just happened!

The view outside the left waist gun window on the Collings Foundation B-24J *Witchcraft.* This was the same view Hank Culver had when his .50 caliber machine gun was ripped out of his hands while he was firing at an enemy plane. Photo taken from a video still taken on August 24, 2013 by the author.

An additional result of the unexploded shell's impact was that the plane's hydraulic and communications' systems were partially knocked out due to the path and concussion of the shell. Thankfully the shell was a dud, otherwise it would've exploded upon impact and killed all aboard. The flight engineer, George Snook, later commented that he believed it was made by slave labor who deliberately sabotaged the shell. Some said that the fuse didn't work. Whatever the case, the jolted crew was incredibly thankful for that, to say the least. With damage to the plane, and over three and half hours of flying time left, the shaken crew had to work together to get the plane, and themselves, safely back to their base in England. There would be more flak batteries to face on the way back, and the threat of enemy fighters. If they did manage to make it back to England, they also had another big problem - getting the landing gear down and using the brakes without full hydraulics. Their problems had just begun…

Left. A German soldier holding an .88mm anti-aircraft high explosive shell. This is what went through the Williams crew's plane, *Nine Yanks and a Jerk*, without exploding. Normally such a shell would explode on impact or at certain altitudes. Right: A German flak battery in 1943. From the websites http://www.ebay.com/itm/GERMAN-88mm-GUN-SHELL and http://en.wikipedia.org/wiki/8.8_cm_Flak.

FOREWARD

Can an airplane embody the American spirit?

The lumbering B-24, "Nine Yanks and A Jerk," certainly symbolizes the resilience and optimism of our nation during a dark time. It was shot at and kept flying. It was hit and kept flying. And then on April 12, 1944, it suffered a final, fatal blow. But the ideals of democracy and freedom that sent it into the air still resonate to this day.

I grew up with the stories of the plane and its crew, as my father was the pilot on its last mission. The plane had been on its way, in formation, to bomb Zwickau, Germany when cloud cover forced the 8th Air Force crews to turn back. As they flew over Belgium, the Messerschmitts caught up with them. Two crew members, Fred Cotron, the radio operator and tail gunner Martin Clabaugh were killed that day when the plane was shot out of the sky. I think of them and what their ultimate sacrifices mean quite often.

I first heard of Scott Culver's book when I visited the crash site in the summer of 2014 in Perwez, Belgium. My wife, son and I were warmly and so touchingly received by Benjamin Heylen and his family, who have created a remarkable museum that is a tribute to the allied war effort that freed their nation from the Nazi grip. They told me that Scott's father, flying close by in his B-24, actually witnessed my father's plane being shot down and that Scott was researching and writing this book.

In 2015, I invited Scott to be a guest with me on Fox News to reflect on the sacrifices of our fathers and their fellow fliers, and on what lessons we could take from their efforts as we face new threats today. The saga of the airplane, and with it, the legacies of our fathers, have now come full circle, generations later.

This book is a vivid reminder of what they faced. "Nine Yanks and A Jerk" took flight against the enemies of freedom. We can use its example today to inspire us to face the challenges of our time. This is a very special and important book.

Eric Shawn, Fox News Anchor and Senior Correspondent, January 20, 2016

On Sunday, November 15, 2015, Fox News host Eric Shawn interviewed the author about the book on his TV program, *America's News Headquarters*. The live broadcast was right after the terrorist attacks in Paris. Eric did a great job of connecting the stories of our fathers' service together in WWII to current events. Images courtesy Fox News.

U.S. President Franklin D. Roosevelt and British Prime Minister Winston Churchill (seated) and their Combined Chiefs of Staff military advisors met in Casablanca in January of 1943. General Henry 'Hap' Arnold, Commanding General of the U.S. Army Air Forces (far left) made the case for U.S. Daylight Precision Bombing with the help of General Ira Eaker (below). Photo courtesy of the FDR Memorial Library.

From January 14th to the 24th of 1943, the Combined Chiefs of Staff (CCS) from the United States and Great Britain, with U.S. President Franklin D. Roosevelt and British Prime Minister Winston Churchill, met in Casablanca, French Morocco to review and further formulate a plan to win the war in Europe.

At the conference, the Allied nations reaffirmed their commitment to the complete destruction of Germany's military, industrial, and economic base, and to decimate the morale of the German people. In relation to air power, the conference issued the Casablanca Directive, which listed priorities for strategic bombing objectives for the American and British air forces. The list of German targets by category was restated from a previous agreement by priority – submarine construction, aviation industry, transportation, fuel production, and many other essential industries that supplied Germany's ability to wage war.

One of the key items of discussion and debate was the issue of whether or not the Americans should continue their strategy of Daylight Precision Bombing, as opposed to the British nightly carpet (or area) bombing, which the British were convinced was less destructive to their air forces due to the cover of darkness. In the weeks leading up to the meetings, U.S. General Henry 'Hap' Arnold was being pressured by senior Royal Air Force officers to join them in the nightly bombing campaign. The British said that the Americans were losing too many bombers and crews during their daylight raids due to enemy fighter attacks and the German anti-aircraft cannons, without showing significant results in the destruction of enemy installations. (This was something the American aircrews knew all too well. The British quite frankly thought that it was impossible.) However, Arnold continued to press for daylight bombing, making the case that the destruction of enemy installations and targets would be more precise, especially as the American air forces grew in number of planes and men, and thus would help to end the war sooner. He also stressed how American aircrews were trained to fly in daylight in order to make use of the more precise top secret Norden Bombsight, which claimed more pinpoint accuracy. To fend off the British insistence, Arnold brought along the commander of the U.S. 8th Air Force (which was based in England), General Ira Eaker.

Eaker presented Arnold with a paper he wrote called, "The Case for Day Bombing," which Arnold used to make persuasive arguments with the British air officers. Eaker eventually won the day by convincing Churchill to agree to their position in a one page paper he presented him with, which included a significant statement, one that fit Churchill's style. In it Eaker wrote, "By bombing the devils around the clock, we can prevent the German defenses from getting any rest." Even though his wording had a humorous and mischievous tone to it, there was a serious, valid strategy to it. The idea was that the two nations could join together in an unrelenting bombing campaign against Germany, and thus win the war by attrition. After some back and forth discussion, Churchill saw Arnold and Eaker's point, changed his mind, and joined with them, even against his own chief air force officers' opinions. (*The Road to Big Week*, Hammel, p.207).

The missions described within this work are a few examples of the many dangers of American Daylight Precision Bombing within the above mentioned directive (which was updated in June of 1943, and given the code name Operation Pointblank. See p.23.). The daily hazards that the American bomber crews faced in those daunting years leading up to the Allied invasion of Europe, and after, are innumerable. The pages contained herein will give the reader a glimpse into the lives and hazards of a few of those brave men who volunteered to be part of the American bomber teams, and how they fulfilled their duty by bringing the war directly to Germany's home turf.

A U.S. Army Air Force bombardier peers through the telescopic lens as he calibrates his top secret Norden Bombsight upon approach to the target. The American bombardiers were especially trained for Daylight Precision Bombing. This is what each American bombing mission was about – getting the bombs on the target as accurately as possible while making use of the better visibility in the daytime. Photo taken from the WWII documentary, *Target for Today* (1944), from the National Archives and Records Administration (*NARA*).

"Daylight Raiders"
Nine Yanks and a Jerk, 703rd Bomb Squadron, 445th Bomb Group, Tibenham, England, 8th Air Force
Raid on Nurnberg, Germany, February 25, 1944

The Mission History

Presumably named to honor its original crew of nine northerners and perhaps one southerner, the Metcalf crew, *Nine Yanks and a Jerk* had been flown by other crews after its original crew had gone down in the North Sea without a trace while flying on another plane that was starting out on the February 2, 1944 mission to Syracourt, France (see p.102). Later, on February 25, 1944, *Nine Yanks and a Jerk*, was flown by Lt. William "Mack" M. Williams' crew as their replacement plane from the same 445th Bomb Group, 703rd Bomb Squadron which was based in Tibenham, England. For some of the crew members it was their 13th mission. They were flying this plane as a replacement because their regular plane, *"Hap" Hazard*, had been battle damaged on a previous mission. They were sent to bomb German aviation industry targets at Furth near Nurnberg, Germany and had to pass through the heavily defended Ruhr Valley to get there with the 2nd Air Division of the 8th Air Force. This was the final mission of the Big Week raids. The Big Week raids were planned by 8th Air Force commander General Jimmy Doolittle (already famous for his raid on Tokyo, Japan in April of 1942) and General Fred Anderson, in order to cripple the Luftwaffe's ability to produce fighter planes and their control of the air war over northwestern Europe. The Williams crew had already flown two other missions previously in the same week to other German aviation industry targets at Brunswick on February 20th and Gotha on the 22nd. It was a terrible battle in the air throughout the week, but well worth it, because the 8th Air Force bombers pounded every one of the German installations they attacked. It also became the turning point in the air war over Europe as Allied fighters not only escorted the heavy bombers all the way to their targets, but were also able to shoot down many of the German fighters that were attacking them. As a result, the Germans began to lose their aerial supremacy in the air war over Europe.

U.S. Eighth Air Force

445th Bomb Group

703rd Bomb Squadron

DEDICATION AND INTRODUCTION

This book is especially dedicated to the courageous airmen of the Williams crew, who served in aerial combat with the 703rd Bomb Squadron in the 445th Bombardment Group, U.S. 8th Air Force based in Tibenham, England in World War II. These men served during the crucial winter and spring of 1943-44, at the height of the air war in Europe. Under the skillful and courageous leadership of their famous squadron commander, James "Jimmy" M. Stewart (of Hollywood and movie fame), these dedicated airmen, along with their fellow airmen from the rest of the 703rd, 700th, and 701st, and 702nd Bomb Squadrons, were one crew among thousands in the U.S. 8th Air Force who helped play a key role in bringing the war to Hitler's doorstep. They helped to dismantle Hitler's empire, brick by brick, literally and figuratively. While their British counterparts bombed Hitler's regime at night, the Americans remained committed to the doctrine of Daylight Precision Bombing at a time when its success was still in question back in the States, as well as by the crews in air combat over Hitler's "Fortress Europe."

The Williams crew, along with their fellow 8th Air Force crews, were originally required to fly 25 combat missions. The completion rate for a crew to finish its 25 missions was less than 25%. Chances were that they might either have been killed in the air, shot down and taken prisoner, been killed by angry German citizens if they survived a bail out, or spend weeks or months evading capture on the Continent. With the introduction of the American P-51 Mustang fighter plane into the European Theater of Operations, those odds increased in favor of a crew completing its 25 missions. The P-51 was a game-changer in the battle for aerial supremacy over the skies of Europe. Because of its speed and maneuverability, and the skills of its well-trained pilots, it out-performed the best German fighters at the time. As additional fuel drop tanks were developed for the P-51s, and also for the P-47s and P-38s, the result was that these fighter planes were able to escort the bombers all the way to Berlin and back to their bases in England. The American fighter pilots flying these planes were also allowed flexibility in their bomber escort duties in order to pursue the German fighter planes both in the air and on the ground, destroying them at every opportunity. The Williams crew witnessed the introduction of the fantastic P-51 Mustang into their theater of operations. Because of the success and supremacy gained in aerial combat by these fighters, by mid-April of 1944, the 8th Air Force upped the tour of duty requirements for its bomber crews to 30 missions, instead of 25. Even with the long-range protection of the P-51s, along with the P-38s, P-47s, and British Spitfires, many bomber crews still did not complete their 30 missions.

The Williams crew was only one of six crews to complete their 30 missions from the squadron's original 16 planes that left the United States in November of 1943 and arrived in England to serve in combat. All of the crew members on this crew knew that it was against all odds that they would finish their tour of duty. (Co-pilot Douglas Pillow, who was wounded about halfway through his tour of duty when he was piloting his own plane with a new crew, completed 18 missions up to that point) Some would say it was by the grace of God, other included luck and chance in the equation. There was also no doubt that it was also due to their diligence and skills as an excellent crew. The additional fact that they often flew as part of the first three lead planes into their targets was a key factor, as that was one of the safer positions in a flight formation. Many German fighter pilots looked to pick off the 'tail-end Charlies' – bombers that were at the tail ends of formations, or ones losing air speed and thus could not keep up with the group formation.

My father always said that he often knew and felt that it was not his time to die during his tour of duty. Even though there were moments of doubt and fear, he frequently commented that he somehow sensed that his time was not yet up. He also said that his crew all got along very well together, and they did their jobs with diligence. They also were thankful to survive the harrowing, near death experiences they often encountered (thus showing a strong will to live). This book is a retelling of one segment of their story. It is the accounting of one of their most dangerous missions taken from U.S Army Air Force records, personal diaries and letters, their own eyewitness accounts, as well as interviews with surviving family members. It is also a tribute to their very competent, unfailing, and well-beloved squadron commander, Major James Stewart. Through the trials and dangers of war, Jimmy Stewart lived up to and exceeded his onscreen character portrayals they all knew him so well for. He truly led by example.

The nose turret was washed out in the photo because it was top secret.

445TH BOMBARDMENT GROUP (HEAVY), 703RD BOMB SQUADRON
THE B-24 CREW OF "HAP HAZARD" ✦ THE WILLIAMS' CREW
TOP ROW (LEFT TO RIGHT): 2ND LT. WILLIAM "MACK" WILLIAMS (PILOT), 2ND LT. DOUGLAS PILLOW (COPILOT), 2ND LT. JESSE CUMMINGS (NAVIGATOR), 2ND LT. JACK HEANY (BOMBARDIER), TECH/SGT. GEORGE SNOOK (ENGINEER) BOTTOM ROW (LEFT TO RIGHT): S/SGT. JOE MINTON (TAIL GUNNER), S/SGT. BILLY FIELDS (RIGHT WAIST GUNNER), TECH/SGT. FRANK MANGAN (RADIO OPERATOR), MASTER/SGT. GRANT MURRAY (GROUND CREW CHIEF/NON-FLYING), S/SGT. HENRY "HANK" CULVER (BALL TURRET & WAIST GUNNER), S/SGT. HENRY GOING (LEFT WAIST GUNNER)

The Williams crew flew *Nine Yanks and a Jerk* on a mission to bomb Nurnberg, Germany on February 25, 1944. Here they're pictured on October 7, 1943, in front of their original plane, *'Hap' Hazard*, at Sioux City Army Air Base in Sioux City, Iowa just before their overseas deployment to their base at Tibenham Airfield, England. At Sioux City they met the famous movie actor-turned bomber pilot, Captain Jimmy Stewart, who became their new squadron commander in the 703rd Bomb Squadron with the 445th Bomb Group. Stewart led the group to their overseas station via Nebraska, Florida, Puerto Rico, British Guiana, two stops in Brazil, Senegal, Morocco and then to England. The crews who knew Stewart had only good things to say about their commanding officer.

AIRCREW POSITIONS ON A B-24 LIBERATOR HEAVY BOMBER

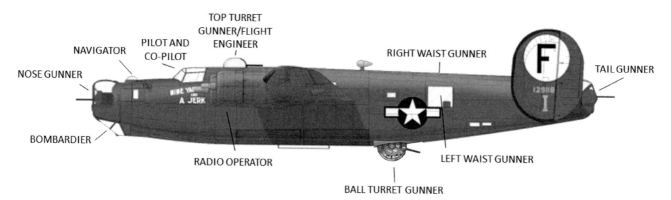

Image courtesy of Bob Migliardi at Iliad Design.

The above diagram illustrates the aircrew combat positions of a B-24H or J model Liberator heavy bomber (the "B" stands for "Bomber"). The earlier B-24D model (p.61) did not have a nose turret, but a glass nose with a few machine guns sticking out through holes fitted within the glass. The 445th Bomb Group flew combat with the new top secret nose turret, which was more deadly and could better ward off frontal attacks by German fighters.

The Williams crew trained together for over five months in the States and a few weeks in England before entering combat over northwest Europe. They flew most of their 30 missions together in these positions from mid-December of 1943 through the end of June of 1944, during Operations Pointblank and Argument (p.23-26).

In WWII, a heavy bomber had four engines, could carry a heavier payload and fly longer distances than a twin-engine medium bomber, such as the B-25 Mitchells or the B-26 Marauders (see Appendix p. 142). The B-24 Liberators and the B-17 Flying Fortresses were the two main U.S. heavy bombers during the war. The B-29 Superfortress (designated Very Heavy) saw most of its service in the Pacific in the last year and a half of WWII.

B-24H/J Liberator Specifications

Engines	Four 1,200-hp Pratt & Whitney R-1830-65 Twin Wasp turbocharged radial piston engines.
Weight: Empty	36,500 lbs
Max Overload Takeoff	71,200 lbs
Wing Span	110ft.
Wing Area	1048 sq. ft.
Length:	67ft. 2in.
Height	18ft.
Performance	Maximum Speed at 25,000 ft: 290 mph Cruising Speed: 215 mph Ceiling: 28,000 ft. Range: 2,100 miles
Armament	10 x .50 caliber machine guns in nose, top turret, ball turret and tail turret, and on two sides.
Bomb Load	8800 lbs.

THE BIG PICTURE – OPERATION POINTBLANK

"It's a conceded fact that Overlord [the cross-Channel invasion]
will not be possible unless the German Air Force is destroyed."
General Henry H. Arnold, Commander of the U.S. Army Air Forces, December 27, 1943

General Henry H. Arnold

In order to clear the skies of enemy aircraft over the invasion beaches of northern France for Operation Overlord in the spring of 1944, the USSTAF (United States Strategic and Tactical Air Forces in Europe, which included the U.S. Eighth and Ninth Air Forces in England and the U.S. Fifteenth Air Force in Italy), commanded by General Carl Spaatz, was given the enormous task of destroying Germany's industrial capabilities. Its target was especially its aviation industry, as well as the German Luftwaffe. The big vision for these strategic attacks was given the code name Operation Pointblank. It had been in the planning stages since the directive was given in June of 1943. The directive was a result of the Casablanca Conference held in Casablanca, Morocco in January of 1943, and was approved by the orders of U.S. President Franklin D. Roosevelt and British Prime Minister Winston Churchill who were in attendance there. Working together, the Allied air forces were ordered to destroy the Luftwaffe wherever they could find it – in the air and on the ground, which also included assembly plants. The British Royal Air Force (RAF) would bomb the same targets during the night to add to the destruction of the enemy's ability to fight in the air, and to give the enemy less time to rebuild. Some of the key German aircraft factories to be bombed were the Messerschmitt factory at Regensburg, along with the ball-bearing factory at Schweinfurt on August 17, 1943. Schweinfurt was bombed again in October. Those raids resulted in heavy losses of American bombers and crews (60 B-17s and crews on both raids), with little consolation for target damage compared to American losses.

In addition to heavy combat losses, the fall and winter of 1943-44 did not have a whole lot of good flying and bombing weather, due to overcast skies and poor visual bombing opportunities. The conditions over those regions had been quite unpredictable and was covered with much overcast for extended periods between October 1943 and early February of 1944. In addition, the U.S. Eighth Air Force was taking a beating from the Luftwaffe because the Allied friendly fighters, the American P-38 Lightnings, P-47 Thunderbolts, P-51 Mustangs, and British Spitfires were not able to escort the heavy bombers all the way to their targets deep in Germany due to the fighters' limited fuel loads. The fighters were not equipped with enough fuel space to take them all the way to those distant targets and back to England. As a result, the German Air Force was shooting down large numbers of the American bombers who were left to defend themselves over German airspace. Even though the bombers were equipped with ten .50 caliber machine guns, the bombers and their crews were like sitting ducks in the sky

General Carl A. Spaatz

as the German fighter pilots dove in, strafing the American bomber formations at will. The German fighter pilots, known for their head-on attacks, were having a field day. There were no foxholes in the sky for the American aircrews to hide themselves in. They desperately needed fighter escorts that could protect them all the way to their targets and back in order to reduce their losses and increase their bombing effectiveness. They would, however, get this coverage in early 1944.

General Arnold's 1944 New Year's message to his Eighth and Fifteenth Air Force commanders concluded as follows – "This is a MUST - Destroy the Enemy Air Force wherever you find them, in the air, on the ground and in the factories." The besetting predicament, in the winter of early 1944, was that the American air forces needed a good week of clear weather over Germany to begin effective, decisive, and devastating strikes at the heart of German aviation industry - factories, airfields, and assembly plants in central and southern Germany. The clear weather would also give the American fighter pilots the opportunity to attack the German fighters in the air. Added fuel tanks would allow for this by giving them a deeper range into German air space. The coordination of all of this would take skillful, painstaking planning, and patience. For those flying, it would take a lot of courage, nerves, and stamina.

BIG WEEK – OPERATION ARGUMENT

The long-awaited concentrated plan of attack finally became a reality in late February of 1944. The week of missions was secretly known as Operation Argument – which was be an all-out combined Allied aerial assault against German aviation industry and the Luftwaffe. Operation Argument, which fit within the framework of Operation Pointblank, had been in the planning stages since November of 1943, but had suffered set-backs due to the above mentioned reasons.

Around the time when General James "Jimmy" Doolittle took charge of the U.S. Eighth Air Force in England in January of 1944 (having replaced Eaker), General Henry Arnold, the Commander of the U.S. Army Air Forces, had hand-picked a weather expert, Major Irving P. Krick, from Cal Tech in the United States to work with him. Krick was called in to make accurate weather predictions and calculations, so that the Americans could effectively plan their daylight bombing missions. Krick had a unique approach to weather forecasting, which was not shared by many of his contemporaries. Krick's strategy was to research European weather patterns over the last century, and see how those patterns reoccurred over time. He

General James "Jimmy" H. Doolittle

believed that there were certain weather conditions that repeated themselves in predictable measures. Krick, although ridiculed by his cronies who were using conventional methods, deduced from his studies that there would be a clearing pattern over northern Europe, especially over Germany, during the third week of February of 1944. In contrast to all appearances, and the scorn of his skeptics, it turned out that he was right.

In addition, General Fred Anderson, who served under Spaatz as his Operations Officer, was also receiving Allied reports (that were deciphered from a German weather station in Krakow, Poland) that a windy, high pressure front was moving out of the Baltic into Germany for a week of clear, cold weather – ideal for visual bombing. Anderson pressed for Operation Argument to take place as he received confirmation for good weather on

General Fredrick L. Anderson

February 19th. From February 20th through the 25th, the long awaited week of clear weather over central and southern Germany had arrived. For those reasons, the week of Operation Argument would later become known as Big Week, and would mark the turning point in the air war over Europe. It would also turn out to be one of the biggest and most important periods in aerial warfare history, ever.

Doolittle, although having some reservations himself, planned accordingly from his headquarters (code named "Pinetree") located at High Wycombe in England. The plans were made in the former girl's school known as Wycombe Abbey. The great aerial armada's headquarters lay in the British countryside about 30 miles northwest of Charing Cross in central London. As the afternoon of February 19, 1944 arrived, the weather in England didn't look promising. Doolittle and his commanders saw the country socked in with cloud cover and light rains. Even if the weather over the European continent was clear, ordering his heavy bombers to take-off in heavy overcast and rain from their bases in England could be disastrous because of ice build-up on the wings, possible mid-air collisions, and pilots not being able to find their formations as they were ascending through the cloud cover. Doolittle, known as the master of the calculated risk, decided to go ahead as planned and took advantage of the weather over the European continent, even though England's airspace was problematic. It was the beginning of what would be a six day strategic bombing campaign, and a well-calculated risk.

Between February 20th and the 24th, the U.S. Army Air Forces had five continuous days of American Daylight Precision Bombing. This was also coupled with the British nightly attacks. As a result, the Allied air forces pounded key strategic aviation targets in Germany all that week. The raging aerial confrontations were costly to both the Allied and Axis forces. Hundreds of men and planes were lost on both sides in the fierce air battles over the Nazi homeland and occupied lands. Many of the bomber crews and fighter pilots who had made it back from those missions also felt the stress and fatigue of flying back to back days of combat. Although the damage done by Allied bombing was extensive, it was not crippling. Even so, the Allies were making a good dent in the Luftwaffe's ability to fight back and replenish their forces. The Luftwaffe also lost some of its best and most seasoned fighter pilots that week.

Many of Doolittle's advisors were against planning one more mission that week, due to the stress already placed on the American airmen and machines that flew those missions, as well as the ground crews who were working around the clock to keep the damaged planes repaired and flyable. Nevertheless, Doolittle decided to go ahead with one more mission that week. He would show Adolf Galland (the German Luftwaffe officer in charge of Germany's fighter defense network) who would now control the skies over Europe. Not wanting the opportunity of one more day of clear weather over Germany to pass by, Doolittle once again ordered the Eighth Air Force bomber and fighter groups into the air one last time that week for another major assault on Hitler's aviation industry and Galland's Luftwaffe pilots. With the Allied invasion (Operation Overlord) planned for the spring, Doolittle knew that he had only three months left to cripple Germany's Air Force, so that any planes seen over the invasion beaches on D-Day would only be Allied ones.

On the evening of February 24th, Doolittle gave the orders to plan for the final mission of that historic week. Another huge aerial armada of American bombers and fighters would be on their way to annihilate carefully considered targets in Germany. The phones began ringing across the American bomber and fighter bases late that evening. The teletype machines were chattering away and printing out the information needed for the Combat Wings and their Bomb Groups (along with their squadrons) to begin their all night planning for the mission that would begin early the next morning.

The sixth and final mission of Big Week was about to begin. For one more day in that historic week in aerial warfare history the U.S. Eighth Air Force (as part of the U.S. Army Air Forces) would continue its unrelenting bomber and fighter attacks against Nazi Germany, and would show once and for all who would command the skies over Europe. My father, Henry "Hank" Culver, Sr., along with his crew - the Williams crew, continued on that day to be part of one of the greatest aerial assaults in history.

Top l.: A photo taken of a B-24, **Consolidated Mess**, from the 732ⁿᵈ BS, 453ʳᵈ BG, 8ᵗʰ AF on the February 21, 1944 mission to bomb the airfield at Achmer, Germany. This photo was taken by the 445ᵗʰ's sister bomb group the 453ʳᵈ. The picture shows the vapor trails of fighter planes above the bomber formations. The snapshot captures the intensity of aerial battles over the skies of northwestern Europe during the Big Week missions. Operation Argument was in its second day when this dramatic photo was taken. My father and his crew knew these kinds of scenes all too well during those concentrated aerial assaults. Top r.: P-38 Lightnings in formation. These early American twin-engine, twin-tailed fighters were often seen escorting the American bombers over Europe. *NARA* Bottom: A close-up of a P-38 at McGuire Air Force base in New Jersey in 2012. Author's collection. The author in front of a P-38 at The National Museum of the U.S. Air Force at Wright-Patterson Air Force Base, Ohio in 2014.

Note: The terms U.S. Army Air Corps (USAAC) and U.S. Army Air Force or Forces (USAAF) were used interchangeably by many airmen during the war. They are used interchangeably within this work also. However, the U.S. Army Air Corps officially became the U.S. Army Air Forces in June of 1941. Men who entered the air arm of the U.S. Army early in the war often referred to their branch as the Air Corps. This is often how my father referred to his branch, even though he enlisted in November of 1942, a year and a half after its new designation. The U.S. Air Force became its own separate branch of the U.S. military in 1947, two years after World War II.

THE AMERICAN BOMBER BASE AND AIRFIELD AT TIBENHAM, ENGLAND

In the pre-dawn hours of Friday, February 25, 1944, a sergeant CQ (Charge of Quarters) pulled up in his jeep with dimmed, black-painted headlights to the Site 5 Nissen hut area at the American heavy bomber base at Tibenham Airfield. The dimmed headlights were to prevent enemy aircraft from spotting the air base in the early morning hours while it was still dark. The 703rd Bomb Squadron's enlisted aircrews were quartered at this site, which was about a half a mile from the runway at the northeastern edge of the base, and about a mile east of the village of Tibenham in rural Norfolk County, England. There was light sporadic rain over the base. The bare trees scattered around the huts stood silently like silhouetted sentinels over the sleeping airmen in the dead of winter. The tall trees also lined the edges of the air base property near centuries old hedgerows. The hedgerows marked the boundary lines of local farms that had been around just as long. They also served to mark off the different Nissen hut sites where the airmen were quartered. It was an illustration in contrast – a sleepy rural area in England where the sounds of war were about to stir the quiet air in the still English countryside. The air base, which was about eighty miles (one hundred and twenty-eight km) northeast of London and thirteen miles (twenty-one km) southeast of Norwich, was one of over 100 American airdromes in the huge agricultural region of East Anglia that was waking up to another day's combat mission.

Tibenham Airfield was a former RAF airfield which dated back to World War I. It was built up and expanded in 1942 to accommodate the four-engine, heavy bombers that were soon to arrive. It would be one of over 100 such American bases built in East Anglia and across Britain in order to bring the war to Nazi occupied Europe, just across the North Sea and the English Channel.

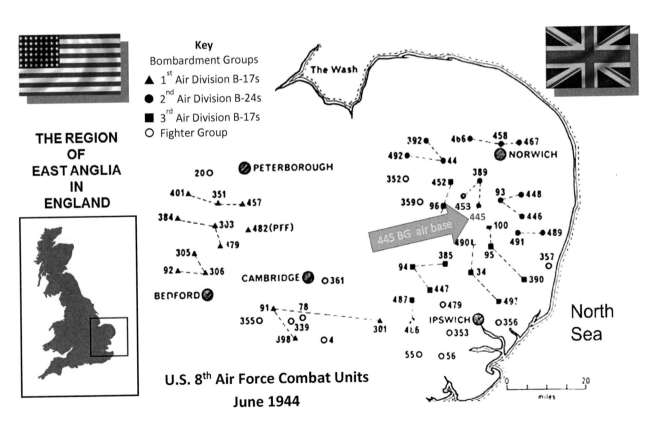

The U.S. 8th Air Force Combat Units and their Combat Wings (connected),
Air Divisions, and Fighter Units in East Anglia by June of 1944.

Located near its namesake, the centuries old English village of Tibenham, the airfield's American personnel increased the village's population practically overnight by over 3,000 people when 'the Yanks' arrived there in October and November of 1943. Prior to the war, the village had a local population under 1,000. It was quite an abrupt mixing of American and British cultures as a result. In spite of some differences, lifelong relationships would also be forged between the two nations because of the war.

The planes flown from this base were the four-engine B-24 Liberators, the most produced plane in American history. Over 18,000 of the heavy bombers had been built during the war. Dozens of such planes were scattered throughout the airfield's 51 dispersal points and two huge T-hangars to protect them from an enemy fighter or bomber attack. The same was true for the quarters of the enlisted men and officers, as they too were up to a half mile away from the runways to avoid an easy attack, should one occur.

The mission would be the 445th Bomb Group's twenty-ninth combat mission since flying their first operation on December 13, 1943, when they bombed the submarine pens at Kiel, Germany. Waking the group's aircrews in the early hours of the morning for a mission had become routine by this time. The sound of the jeep's engine and its squealing brakes woke some of the crews up even before the CQ entered their huts with his flashlight and unwelcomed voice. The typical moans and groans were heard from the men as they struggled to rise from their winter slumber and take a deep breath of the cool air inside their barely heated hut. Some of the men were buried under several layers of blankets in order to stay warm. The airmen's huts were like sleeping in a tin can cut in half with two cement ends. The small pot-bellied stoves in the middle of the airmen's hovels were never sufficient to heat the 12-man shelters.

One of the Williams crew's enlisted men standing outside their Nissen hut - Technical Sergeant George Snook (flight engineer and top turret gunner). Tibenham was quite a muddy place when the crews first arrived there. Not all of the hut sites had concrete walkways finished by the time they had arrived. The men's muddy boots can be seen in the background against the hut. Despite the conditions, it was the enlisted men's 'home away from home' for the nine months they were together as a crew in England. These men resided here from November of 1943 through early August of 1944. This photo was probably taken in late 1943 or early 1944. From Hank Culver's collection.

Tibenham Airfield in 2012. The author was flown in a glider tow plane around the airfield by Tony Griffiths, a member of the Norfolk Gliding Club based at the airfield today. The airfield retains most of its WWII configuration. The view is looking west from over the top of the main rail line which runs from Norwich to London, as we were flying south. The countryside is very much the same as in WWII. Author's collection.

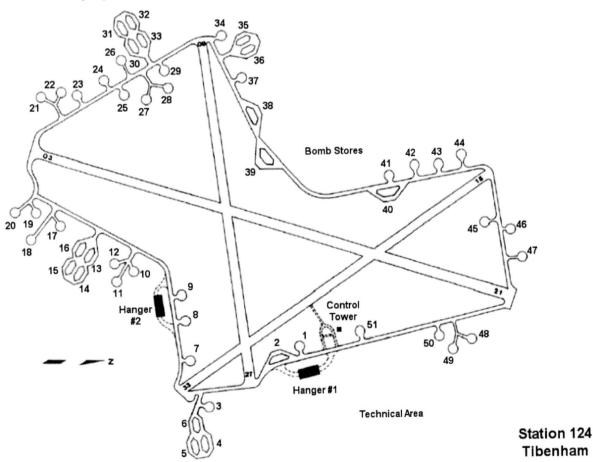

Station 124
Tibenham

Map courtesy of Mike Simpson, www.445BG.org

29

The Williams crews' huts sites on the northeastern edge of the airfield. Photo courtesy Mike Page.

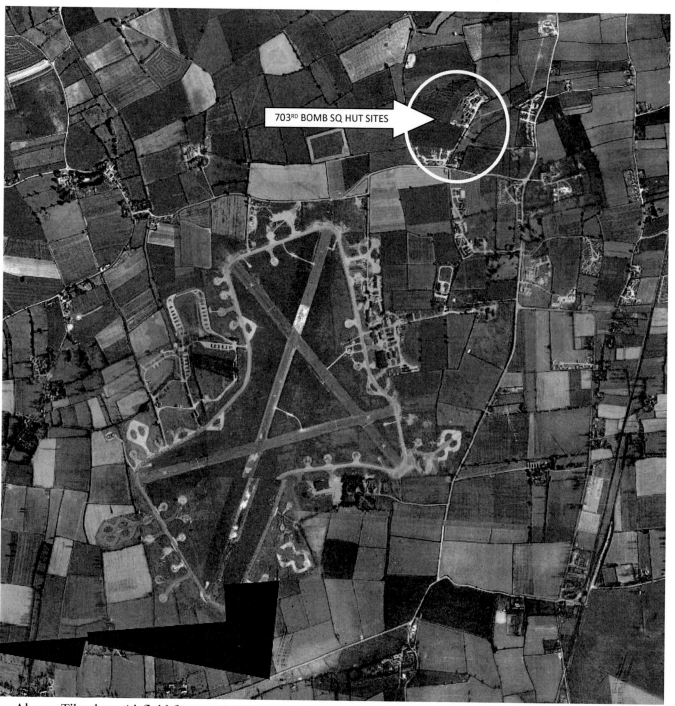

Above: Tibenham Airfield from a 1946 Royal Air Force Aerial Survey photograph. (Note portions missing.)
From the website http://historic-maps.norfolk.gov.uk/mapexplorer

Tibenham Airfield in 2007, very much as it looks today. It is now the home of the Norfolk Glider Club.
Photo courtesy of Mike Page.
Below: A view from the west looking east on June 30, 2012. Author's collection

THE WILLIAMS CREW

As the sergeant entered the Williams enlisted crew's hut, he gave some of the crew members a little shove to jostle them awake. Some cursed the sergeant out loud, some under their breath, others just in their thoughts. A few even felt like shooting him with their .45 caliber pistols for getting them up before the roosters. "The Williams crew… you're flying today," was heard as he entered hut number 2 around 4:30 AM, which was followed by his announcement that their briefing time would be at 5:30 AM. The early wake-up call was the usual practice for getting the crews ready for an early morning take-off. It seemed like they had just gone to sleep, and now it was time to get up before daylight. Some of the men didn't get to bed until 11:00 PM the night before. Take-off time for the Williams crew was 9:33 AM.

My father, S/Sgt. Henry "Hank" J. Culver, Sr., in front of his Nissen hut at Tibenham Airfield, England in late 1943 or early 1944.

Getting ready for a day's mission took several hours of preparation. There wasn't even time to start a new fire in the pot-bellied stove in their hut, nor was it worth it, as they had to make haste to get to the mess hall, and then to the briefing room. Showering usually was done the evening before because the water and air temperatures were too cold in the morning. The shower water was usually cool any time, day or night. The same scenario was unfolding for the rest of the 703rd Squadron and the three other squadrons' crews – the 700th, 701st, and 702nd - at their huts sites scattered around the airfield. The officers, in their quarters at Site 6 (about a half a mile away), did not escape the same process either. Instead of twelve men to a hut, the officers had eight.

The Williams crew[1] enlisted members were as follows. Technical Sergeant George Snook, the flight engineer and top turret gunner was from Ashland, Ohio. After George graduated high school in 1939, he worked in a print shop until he was drafted in October of 1942. George had developed an interest in planes at Ashland Airport. He had wanted to sign up with the Air Corps, but was drafted before he could do that. He took a mechanical aptitude test and wound up transferring to the Air Corps anyhow. He also took another test and qualified as a gunner. Technical Sergeant Frank Mangan, the radio operator from Binghamton, New York, graduated high school in 1938. He enlisted just two months after Pearl Harbor. Frank had worked with his father in the composing room at the Binghamton Sun Press newspaper for a year and a half before enlisting. He had also worked as a serviceman in a tire company business. He had originally wanted to go into the medical corps because he and a friend had also gained some experience working in a pharmacy before the war. Frank eventually took an aptitude

1. A more extensive biography section for each crew member is in the larger work, *Daylight Raiders*.

test to become a radio operator.

Staff Sergeant Henry "Hank" Culver, the ball turret and occasional left waist gunner and assistant engineer, was from Jersey City, New Jersey. Born in Queens, New York, Hank was raised in Queens, Brooklyn, and Manhattan during his childhood. He left high school six months before graduation in order to work with his mother and sister in New York City in Russek's, a high end women's apparel store, to help make ends meet. He moved to Jersey City, New Jersey in 1940. He then worked for Western Electric in Kearney, New Jersey as a clerk typist in payroll for about a year prior to his enlistment. Seeing that the draft age was being lowered from 21 to 18 in November of 1942, Hank enlisted in the Air Corps, rather than get drafted into the ground Army. He later went to aircraft mechanics school and gunnery school after passing aptitude tests. Staff Sergeant Billy Fields, the right waist gunner and armorer (one who armed the bombs), was from Ironton, Ohio. After Billy graduated

from high school in 1940, he attended Indiana Technical College in Fort Wayne, Indiana for two years. In December of 1942, he received his notice for induction. In January of 1943, he was inducted into the Army. He eventually switched over to the Air Corps and was trained as an armorer and as a gunner.

Staff Sergeant Joe Minton, the tail gunner and another armorer, was from Denham Springs, Louisiana. After graduating high school in 1940, Joe tried a semester of college, but realized it wasn't for him. With jobs being scarce, he and some friends enlisted in the Air Corps in January of 1941. He was assigned various jobs at various bases for a couple of years, and by January of 1943, he was being trained in all kinds of firearms. Later that year, he was trained as a gunner and as an armorer. Staff Sergeant Henry Going, was another gunner and armorer from Chester, South Carolina. While living in Chester, Henry completed only one year of high school. He worked on a 300 to 400 acre farm that his family owned. He enlisted in the U.S. Army Air Corps in October of 1942, and eventually was trained as an airplane mechanic and as an armorer/engineer, and later qualified as a gunner.

The four officers of the Williams crew were as follows. The pilot was 1st Lieutenant William "Mack" M. Williams (not to be confused with the famous radio

1st Lt. William "Mack" Williams at Tibenham Airfield. Mack had just finished 'dry cleaning' his jacket in aviation fuel near the flight line. Photo taken by and courtesy of George Snook.

announcer at the time, William B. Williams) from Coral Gables, Florida. Mack was the only married man on the crew who had a son, Sandy, with his wife Kay. Sandy was a little over a year and a half old. Mack graduated high school in 1934, and joined the Florida National Guard the following year. He worked various jobs before the war, and was a salesman for the Kellogg's food company just before his enlistment into the Army Air Corps in May of 1942. Mack had been taking private pilot flying lessons prior to his enlistment. Once his recruiter heard this, he set him on a fast track to become a pilot in the

LIFE AROUND THE ENLISTED CREW'S NISSEN HUT AT TIBENHAM
WINTER AND SPRING OF 1944

Top left: Hank Culver and George Snook. Top right: Hank Culver, Billy Fields, and Frank Mangan.
Bottom left: Joe Minton, Hank Culver, and Frank Mangan. Bottom right: Henry Going.
Photos taken by George Snook, from Hank Culver's and Frank Mangan's collections.

Army Air Corps. Mack was shocked at this because he had not even soloed yet as a private pilot. Nevertheless, that is what he became in the military. Next, 2nd Lieutenant Douglas Pillow, the co-pilot, was from Paragould, Arkansas. Doug and a couple of friends joined the Army Air Corps in August of 1940. Knowing that war was coming, he and his friends wanted to make their way into the branch of the military they desired before a draft board decided it for them, or before the flood of enlistments kept them from their preferences. He and his friends hitched a ride on a freight train to Chanute Field in Rantoul, Illinois to join the Air Corps there. Doug eventually took a pilot's test to see if he could become one. He passed the test and then went on to flight school to become a bomber pilot.

The navigator, 2nd Lieutenant Jesse Cummings, was from Jasper, Texas. After graduating from high school in 1938, Jesse went to college for a year, then worked in a saw mill for a while, and then went back to college before enlisting in the Army in February of 1942. He tried flight school, but washed-out after an instructor didn't like one of his landings. He later trained as both a bombardier and a navigator in late 1942 and early 1943. The bombardier, 2nd Lieutenant John "Jack" Heany, was from Brooklyn, New York. Jack had enlisted in the Air Corps in the New York National Guard in 1936 at the age of 15, while he was still in high school. In January of 1941, Jack was inducted into full-time service in the Army Air Corps. By late 1942 and early 1943, Jack was trained (like Jesse Cummings) with a dual rating of bombardier and navigator. He and Jesse had met each other at one of these schools.

The officer's ages ranged from Williams at age 27 to Cummings who was 22. The enlisted men were between 20 and 23 years old, Mangan and Snook being the oldest at 23, and Culver the youngest at age 20. In total, the crew was made up of five 'northerners' and five 'southerners' (as they often jokingly put it), all of whom got along very well and were rated as an excellent crew. Since the crew was formed at Gowen Field in Boise, Idaho the previous July, they had been flying hundreds of hours together. They trained for about a month together at Gowen Field, then a month and a half at Pocatello Army Air Base, also in Idaho. From there they were assigned to the 703rd Bomb Squadron with the 445th Bomb Group at Sioux City Army Air Base in Iowa for their final training phase. From the sunny hot deserts of Idaho to the overcast, damp climate of England, they made up their ten-man bomber crew - a band of brothers in the air, through thick and thin.

As the six enlisted men and four officers from the Williams crew muttered and then crawled out from under the stratum of blankets they were entombed in, it seemed like they could never get warm enough in the damp, cold climate of East Anglia. It was quite a change from the sun and warmth they knew only months before. The dampness seemed to remain in their bones. (George Snook remarked years later how he felt like the dampness never left his bones until he returned to the States after the war in Europe was over.) The men put their sock-covered feet on the damp, cold floor of the hut. It was cold, even in their socks. They sluggishly got dressed, put on their heavy fleece-lined B-3 bomber jackets, grabbed their winter hats, and emerged from their frozen metal-roofed huts. It was typically around 32°F (0°C) at this time of morning. They looked like shadows moving through the darkness of the early English morning in the blackout of the air base. Some had flashlights to help see where they were walking. They had to keep the lights pointed downward so as not to let the occasional enemy plane see any beams of light projected into the night sky. An enemy plane, if it were flying below the cloud cover, could easily spot a flashlight beam, which could spell disaster for the air base.

The groggy airmen walked across Tibenham Road, which was now bustling with airmen, vehicles, and bicycle traffic heading towards different points throughout the air base to gear up for the

Above: One of the mess halls at Tibenham. Courtesy of the Norfolk Glider Club Collection. Below: A photo from another air base in England shows how the aircrews were loaded into two and a half ton trucks and jeeps to be taken out to their planes at the dispersal hardstand areas all around the airfield. *NARA*

day's mission.

They blended in with other crews as they walked down the gravel lane that was directly across from their quarters. Passing the coal dump and base theater on the left, they wondered what the mission would be like. Aside from walking, some men could be seen riding bikes over to the mess hall and briefing areas, others caught rides in trucks or jeeps. There wasn't too much conversation. It was mostly quiet contemplation about what was in store for them. Dozens of fellow airmen made their way to the chow line at the mess hall. For a few of the airmen on the Williams crew – Mack Williams, George Snook, Frank Mangan, Billy Fields, and Jesse Cummings - it would be their 13th mission. (Hank Culver, for one, had missed an earlier mission with the crew due to a case of frostbite he suffered from on their second mission to Bremen. For him, and the others, this mission was number 12.) Some of the men were a bit superstitious, wondering if the mission would be jinxed. They were just past the halfway point in the 25 mission tour of duty requirement and were understandably getting edgy about it.

Walking outdoors to the dampness in the cold English air was never a pleasant experience. The intermittent light rains over the base, and solid cloud cover over the airfield about a 1,000 feet high made the start of the day even more dismal. It was a far cry from sunny, dry Idaho. Once inside the warm mess hall, the men found the usual breakfast - powdered eggs, bacon, greasy sausages, toast, and coffee - the standard pre-mission meal. At least it was hot, and something to get warmed up by.

The enlisted men had their own mess hall and the officers were in another one just across from the enlisted men. The talk of all 170 men around their breakfast tables was filled with guesses about where they might be going today. Their conversations were echoed by over 7,500 airmen at other American bases in the mess halls throughout the English countryside that morning who also would be on their way to Germany in the over 750 bombers scheduled to fly that day. For some men, it was their first mission. For others, it was another one of many already flown. An early rise usually meant a long mission ahead. Wherever it would be, they knew that it was likely to be a rugged mission, as had been the case several times that week already. This was the final mission of the Big Week raids. Deep penetrations into Germany were the standard that week (even the Williams crew had already been to Brunswick on the 20th and Gotha on the 22nd). The men rightly guessed the same for that day.

Many of the men would not talk about, but certainly thought about, the 13 bombers and crews that were shot down the day before on the mission to Gotha. Scores of their fellow airmen were either killed, taken prisoner, or trying to escape German capture as they sat and ate breakfast. The previous day's mission was one of the worst losses suffered by a single bomb group up until that time in the U.S. 8th Air Force. The empty cots in many of their huts were silent reminders of the dangers of daylight bombing raids. The frequent losses of crews and friends left many an airman to ponder and agonize over his own mortality. Bomber bases often seemed like visiting a funeral parlor because of the losses.

In spite of the soggy English weather and the previous day's heavy losses, they would soon find out that this mission would also be designed to take full advantage of the unusually clear weather predicted for that week over the Continent. Missions still had to be flown. Replacement crews were on the way, but not soon enough. In the meantime, any airmen who were available and fit to fly, had to go. They had to make the most of every opportunity in order to destroy the German Air Force and aircraft industry before the invasion, which was just about three months away. It would be the Williams crew's third mission during Big Week, and they were experiencing combat fatigue because of it.

Their commanders were already up and about, getting the day's business in order for the mission. Experienced and skillful leadership was needed for the planning and execution of the task at hand.

THE 445TH BOMB GROUP COMMANDERS

The Group Commander of the 445th Bomb Group was 33 year old Colonel Robert Terrill. Terrill was a West Point graduate and career Army officer who was attached to the Army Air Corps in 1932 upon graduation from the U.S. Military Academy. Terrill earned his wings as a pilot at Kelly Field in San Antonio, Texas in 1934. Prior to his assignment with the 445th Bomb Group, his flying experience included two years at Wheeler Field in Hawaii with the 18th Pursuit Group. After that he was assigned to March Field in California with the 17th Attack Group. By January of 1942, he had become the assistant operations officer for the Fourth Air Force command at Hamilton Field, also in California. He later became its operations officer. Terrill had gained a lot of leadership experience and flying time with the Army Air Force prior to commanding a heavy bomber group.

In November of 1942, Terrill was given command of a provisional group at Davis-Monthan Field in Tucson, Arizona. He stayed in command of the group when it moved to Alamogordo, New Mexico and then to Topeka, Kansas. In March of 1943, he took the group to Cairo, Egypt. He returned to the States shortly thereafter, and was assigned in April of 1943 to command the 382nd Bomb Group based at Pocatello, Idaho. Not long after that he helped form the 445th Bomb Group at Wendover Field, Utah. He then took command of the group, trained it, and led it to its base at Tibenham, England where he commanded it until the following summer. Later, in July of 1944, Terrill went on to become the assistant chief of staff for operations of the 2nd Air Division. In May of 1945, he became deputy chief

Left: Major Paul Schwartz – Deputy Group Commander; Lt. Colonel Robert Terrill – Group Commander; Lt. Col. Malcolm Seashore – Group Executive Officer. Photo taken at Sioux City, Iowa in the summer of 1943. *NARA* Right: Brigadier General James P. Hodges – Commander of the 2nd Bombardment (Air) Division; Brigadier General Theodore "Ted" Timberlake – Commander of the 2nd Combat (Bomb) Wing; Colonel Robert Terrill – 445th Bomb Group Commanding Officer. Photo taken at Tibenham Airfield, England during a tour and inspection of the base by General Hodges in late 1943 or early 1944. All of these men had very colorful histories and careers in the Air Force. *NARA*

of staff for operations of the Eighth Air Force. After the war, he served in many key command positions with SAC (Strategic Air Command). He also flew bombing missions in the Korean War.

Major Paul Schwartz was the Deputy Group Commander, who acted as Group Commander in Col. Terrill's absence whenever he was off of the base. He also flew as group leader on combat missions, and presented many of the crews with various medals for their combat service, including an Air Medal to Jimmy Stewart. Schwartz had a very colorful career in the Army Air Force prior to his assignment with the 445th Bomb Group. He entered the Army Air Corps as a cadet at Randolph Field in Texas in 1938. He then trained to become a fighter pilot. He was temporarily grounded by a fighter group commander and was later assigned to become a bomber pilot after he caused students to run for cover when he jokingly buzzed in a fighter plane his former high school campus at Plant High School in Tampa, Florida. He later remarked that his commander's decision to switch him to bombers probably saved his life. In 1943, Schwartz eventually became the Commanding Officer of the 382nd Bomb Group, the same B-24 Group that Colonel Terrill was once commander of at Pocatello Army Air Base, Idaho. Obviously Terrill and Schwartz knew each other from the base there, and eventually Terrill took Schwartz on board when the 445th BG was formed in 1943. Major Schwartz would eventually lead the 445th BG on the first daylight bombing raid to Berlin on March 3, 1944. Later, he would also become the Chief of Staff Officer of the 96th Combat (Bomb) Wing in the 2nd Air Division in England. He also became the youngest Colonel in the USAAF at the age of 28. After his service overseas, he flew the famous comedians Laurel and Hardy around the US as part of the USO show tours to entertain troops.

The group's executive officer was Lt. Col. Malcolm Seashore. Seashore had been in the officer's reserve corps since 1933 and, with war looming on the horizon, went on active duty in March of 1941. Having originally been involved with coastal artillery with the Army, he switched over to the Air Corps. Seashore eventually was assigned to the 445th BG as its executive officer both in the States and overseas. His job was to manage the group's daily activities regarding administration, maintenance, and logistics. This allowed Col. Terrill to focus on the group's strategic, tactical, and operational aspects. However, not wanting to miss out on combat, Seashore racked up 13 missions to his credit as a volunteer gunner with the 445th. In April of 1945, he became an executive officer with a joint French-American tactical air force unit in France. He had been in France since the September of 1944, and was actively involved with the recovery of secret German Air Force planes like the Me 262 fighter jet and other German aircraft that were covertly brought back to the US for analysis on board the British aircraft carrier *HMS Reaper* in July of 1945. Some of the planes and materials were brought to Wright Field, Ohio for analysis and testing. Seashore also later became involved as a key investigating officer regarding the 'flying disks" reports of 1947-48. During that time, he was originally with Project Sign as chief of Material Command Intelligence Technical Analysis in late 1947 and early 1948 under General Twining's command in the investigation of UFOs, based at Wright Field (later Air Force Base).

THEIR FAMOUS 703RD BOMB SQUADRON COMMANDER

Their famous squadron commander was most likely already awake as the crews were being roused from their sleep. He was none other than Jimmy Stewart, the movie actor-turned bomber pilot. When once questioned why he gave up his lucrative acting career (especially after just having won an Academy Award for best-actor for his role as Mike Conner in the 1940 movie *The Philadelphia Story* playing opposite Cary Grant and Katherine Hepburn), his answer was genuine and to the point – "What's wrong with being patriotic?" He meant what he said. He had come from a lineage of men who served in the U.S. military, including his father and grandfather. Stewart was a graduate of Princeton University before beginning his formal acting career. During that time, he always had a personal interest in aviation. Once his acting career began to take momentum, he was able to afford private flying lessons. His flying time as a private pilot before the war had served him well. It would eventually open a door for him to fly with the Air Corps, which led him to this point in his military service. He had worked his way through the ranks from his enlistment as a private in the Air Corps in March of 1941, right up to an officer and a heavy bomber pilot. However, in 1943, the Army Air Force wanted to keep him stateside as an instructor pilot at Gowen Field in Boise, Idaho flying B-17s. No commander wanted to risk sending a famous movie actor into combat. Stewart would have none of it. He repeatedly asked for a combat assignment. He eventually was given one when a commander at Gowen Field, Colonel Walter "Pop" Arnold, put in a call to Colonel Robert Terrill who was already in command of the 445th Bomb Group, which was then stationed at Sioux City, Iowa. The group was in its Third Phase of

On the move - Capt. James Stewart, the 703rd Bomb Squadron's Commander in the 445th Bomb Group, shown here at Tibenham Airfield, England not too long after the group's arrival at their base. He is seen walking down a path at the base with a mess hall in the background. He was promoted to Major in late January of 1944. Photo courtesy of Norfolk Glider Club, Tibenham Airfield, England.

training, which was its final stage before overseas deployment. Terrill took Stewart on board in August of 1943, and quickly promoted him to a squadron commander. Stewart was then assigned to the 703rd Bomb Squadron at Sioux City, Iowa.

Stewart was the rank of a Captain when the group arrived at Tibenham in late November. He was 35 years old at the time, which made him about 15 years older than the average-aged airmen under his command.

Stewart brought maturity, experience, and his excellent piloting skills to the group. His lanky six-foot-three stature also had him towering over most of the men he served with. His height gave him an added air of authority and leadership. The men looked up to him in more than one way. Many of the men observed that he looked out for them like a mother hen looking out for her chicks, yet with a calm reserve. Stewart very much lived up to and exceeded the personas of his movie characters. Many of his men had seen him in those famous movie roles. He had hit it big as the young, self-sacrificing senator Jefferson Smith in *Mr. Smith Goes to Washington,* or the reserved, strength-under-control character of sheriff Tom Destry in *Destry Rides Again,* both released in 1939. His men now saw him live out those qualities he once portrayed on film in reality. Many an airmen under his command all said what my father had said, "The way you see him in the movies is the way he was in real life – a real man's man."

Stewart worked tirelessly around the clock both at planning and flying the group's combat missions. He was diligent about flying practice missions with his crews in order to make sure that they were ready for combat.

James Stewart (fourth from left, standing) is shown here with a few members of the staff and combat crew airmen of the 703rd Bomb Squadron at Tibenham Airfield in front of one of its B-24 Liberators. The Williams crew bombardier, 1st Lt. John "Jack" Heany is kneeling third from the left. He's dressed similarly as in the Williams aircrew photo. (See photo on p.21).

By the end of January of 1944, he was promoted to a Major, but only after he saw to it that his officers under him got their promotions first, which showed how sincere he was about looking out for the men under his command. Stewart had certainly earned his pilot's wings and the rank of Major, as he had proved by his flying, leadership skills, and courage in combat. He was also a natural leader, whom the men responded well to.

Stewart would eventually finish the war as a full-bird Colonel, having flown at least 20 combat missions himself, most of them with the 445th Bomb Group, the rest with the 453rd and the 389th Bomb Groups. He also became a Wing Commander by the end of the war in Europe, and a well-decorated combat veteran (see p.106). He remained in the U.S. Air Force Reserves until 1968 when he turned 60, and retired as a Brigadier General. He remained with SAC most of that time, while continuing his acting career. Some of his famous post-war films were, *It's a Wonderful Life, Harvey, Call Northside 777, Winchester '73, The Man from Laramie, The Naked Spur, Broken Arrow, The Glenn Miller Story, The Spirit of St. Louis, Strategic Air Command, The Greatest Show on Earth, Rear Window, Vertigo, Anatomy of a Murder, The FBI Story, How the West Was Won, The Man Who Shot Liberty Valance, Shenandoah, Two Rode Together, The Flight of the Phoenix, Cheyenne Autumn, Bandolero!,* and *The Shootist,*

Stewart was flying some of the most dangerous missions of the war, which had some of the higher-ups a bit concerned. His men all respected him as their commander, as a first-rate pilot, and one who was there in the thick of it with them. He would also be leading the group on this day's mission in the lead plane. Mack Williams' crew would be flying as Stewart's left wingman on the mission. The two pilots were no strangers to one another, as Williams and Stewart were good friends and drinking buddies.

Jimmy Stewart with crew members from one of his aircrews from the 703rd Bomb Squadron on January 14, 1944, at their base in Tibenham, England. The crew of the **Lady Shamrock** (standing, l to r) Capt. James Stewart, Capt. Jerry Steinhauser, 1st Lt. John Ranken, Capt. Bill Conley, T/Sgt. Harold Eckelberry, 1st Lt. Gordon Parker; (crouching, l to r) S/Sgt. Piercel Bordon, S/Sgt. Kermit Moon, S/Sgt. Edward Baumgarten and T/Sgt. Pappy Wilson. This was taken after their fifth mission, when they were awarded the Air Medal. The Williams crew also flew on this plane on three different missions. Conley's crew also flew to the right of the Williams crew on the February 25, 1944 mission to bomb Nurnberg, Germany, only on a different plane. Photo courtesy of Harold and Janet Eckelberry. Stewart and this crew once flew together in **Nine Yanks and a Jerk**.

THE TARGET FOR TODAY IS... NURNBERG, GERMANY

After breakfast was over, it was a short walk together as a crew to the briefing room. After checking in with the attendance officer, the young crews, mostly between the ages of 19 and 27, settled into their chairs and benches with their fellow crew members as they faced the big curtain in the front of the room. Once they were all settled, someone shouted "Attention," as the group commander Colonel Robert Terrill and the briefing officer entered the room. After being told to "Rest," the men settled back into their seats and listened attentively for an anxiety provoking briefing. As they waited for the standard opening line from the briefing officer – "The target for today is," – the curtain was pulled back. The mission's target was revealed and stated - "Nurnberg, Germany." Gasps, moans, and groans could be heard from the stunned crews. Some of the men said, "Who was throwing darts today?" in reference to the large pins marking the target areas and routes on the huge map. If they weren't fully awake yet, they were now after hearing the target destination. Some of the men sat with bated breath as they saw the red ribbon stretch across the map of northern Europe from their East Anglian base at Tibenham. The red line went almost straight south over the English Channel, across the French coast, just north of Paris, and then directly east across France, and far into Germany. It was a mission that would take them deeper into Germany than they had ever gone before, just about 50 miles from the Czechoslovakian border on the east. Many of the listeners thought that this was it for them, a mission that many would not return from.

Above and right: Messerschmitt Bf 110s, sometimes called (Me) 110s
Bundesarchiv Photo / CC-BY-SA [CC-BY-SA-3.0-de], via Wikimedia Commons.

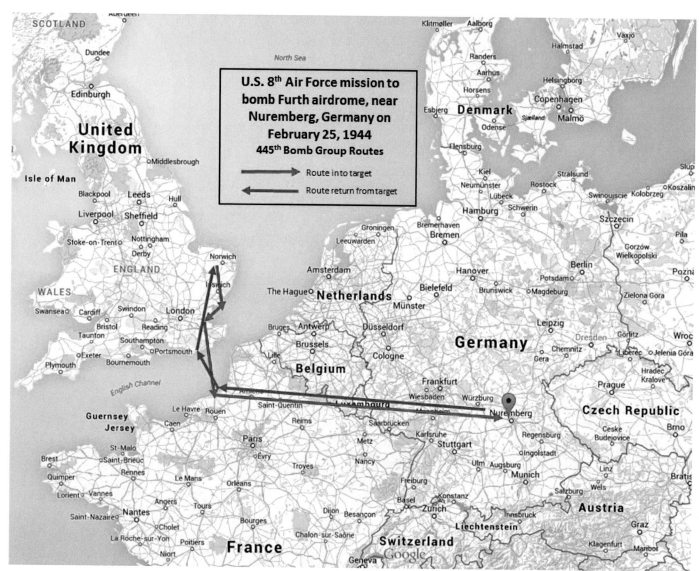

U.S. 8th Air Force mission to bomb Furth airdrome, near Nuremberg, Germany on February 25, 1944
445th Bomb Group Routes
→ Route into target
← Route return from target

The above map shows the routes in and out of the target area. When the aircrews sat in their pre-flight briefing, gasps and moans were heard when the curtain was drawn and the map of their target and the routes were revealed. A few of the men remarked, "Who was throwing darts today?" Those remarks were in response to seeing where the red ribbon on the briefing map had been stretched out to - Nurnberg (a.k.a. Nuremberg), Germany. The 445th Bomb Group, along with other heavy bomb groups, would make its deepest raid into Germany to date. Many of the men didn't think that they would survive it. It would be the closest call for the Williams crew to being blown to pieces than they would ever experience. Google Maps 2015.

Their group's specific mission was to bomb aviation industry targets, including an airfield at Furth, which was a town two miles northwest of Nurnberg (also known as Nuremberg or Nuremburg). The assault would be the 235th Operation the U.S. Eighth Air Force would fly since its operations began in

England in July of 1942. The teletype order for the operation called for a "Maximum Effort," where every bomb group would put up the maximum amount of planes and men that they could from all three heavy bombardment Divisions. Each of the three Divisions had several Combat Wings to them, and each Combat Wing had several Bomb Groups that made them up. It would be an incredibly organized massive offensive. It also meant a lot of round-the-clock work for the planning officers and ground crews who helped ready the aircraft for the day's mission. The operation called for 754 heavy bombers, which included 558 B-17s and 196 B-24s. (See Appendix p.142 for views of a B-17.)

Above: Me 410s. *NARA* and http://www.ww2incolor.com/german-air-force/untitled_002.html

As explained by its Operations officer, the 445th Bomb Group, along with several other B-24 bomb groups from the Second Bombardment Division, was specifically designated to attack the aircraft components and repair factory of Bachman von Blumenthal and Company's aviation buildings and airfield at Furth. The three combat wings of B-24s from the Second Bombardment Division were the Second, Fourteenth, and Twentieth Combat Wings. These three wings would make up the 196 plane raid to destroy what was believed to be the German production of components and the final assembly of Messerschmitt Bf 110s, usually called (Me) 110s. The Me 110 was a twin engine fighter and attack bomber assembled at Brunswick/Waggum and possibly at Gotha, along with Me 410s, another twin-engine fighter and fast bomber that was being used to attack American daylight bombers. The factory was also believed to be engaged in repairing the Me 110s. The square footage of the attack site amounted to 630,000 square feet of floor area. It was a good size target to destroy. It would be the first American bombing raid on this particular target.

The bombers would be escorted by twenty groups of U.S. Army Air Force (USAAF) fighter groups and twelve squadrons of Royal Air Force (RAF) British Spitfires and Mustangs in a "mass penetration of southern Germany to attack three Messerschmitt production centers and an important ball-bearing factory at Stuttgart," according to the *Eighth Air Force narrative of Operations Report, February 25, 1944.*

P-51 Bs and Cs, the early versions of the great WWII fighter plane. These olive drab types entered combat in November of 1943 from their bases in England. The addition of extra fuel tanks, known as 'drop tanks,' under the wings extended their range.

In addition, as stated by another official narrative,

"This was planned as a visual mission [*as opposed to radar guided bombing*] against the Bachmann von Blumenthal & Company aircraft component factory at Furth, Germany. The factory installations were attacked by two Groups of the 14th Combat Wing [*made up of the 44th and 392nd Bomb Groups*] and three groups of the 20th Combat Wing [*which included the 93rd, 446th, and 448th Bomb Groups*]. The factory airfield was attacked by the 2nd Combat Wing [*consisting of the 389th, the 445th, and 453rd Bomb Groups*] carrying maximum load of fragmentation bombs [*which are bombs that exploded into small pieces that traveled at high velocity*]. Sixteen Groups of P-47's, one Group of P-51's, two squadrons of RAF P-51's and ten squadrons of Spitfires furnished overall fighter support for the 1st, 2d, and 3rd, Divisions. One group of P-51's [*from the 357th Fighter Group, the first USAAF fighter group to be equipped with the new P-51 fighter in the 8th AF*] was specifically assigned to this Division for support in the target area. The 458th Group flew a diversion from base to [coordinates] 5500°N-0600°E [over the North Sea, just north of Germany] and return." *Headquarters 2nd Bombardment Division, Tactical Report of Mission, 25 February 1944, dated 15 March 1944.*

One of the few P-51Cs still flying as seen here at the *Warhawk Air Museum* in Nampa, Idaho. Photo taken by author in August of 2013. Courtesy *Warhawk Air Museum.*

Several British Spitfires at the Duxford Airshow at Duxford, England. These versatile, high-performance fighters also escorted American bombers to their targets. Photo taken by the author on July 11, 2015.

I'm in front of the Collings Foundation P-51C at Monmouth Executive Airport in New Jersey in August of 2014. This is the same type of the early P-51s that my father and his group saw in combat in the late part of 1943 and early 1944, only with olive drab paint schemes for camouflage purposes.

The three Bombardment Divisions (later called Air Divisions) that would make up the mission were as follows: the First Bombardment Division, which flew B-17 Flying Fortresses (the sister four-engine bomber to the B-24 Liberators), would fly to Augsburg and Stuttgart, Germany; the Second Bombardment Division, which flew B-24s, would fly to Furth, near Nurnberg, Germany; and the Third Bombardment Division, which also flew B-17s, would fly to Regensburg, Germany. The mission would entail multiple attacks on the enemy's aircraft industry. The various attacks would also help divide the Luftwaffe's aerial assaults against the bomber formations, thus giving the bombers a better chance of hitting their targets, as well as increasing their chances of survival. It was the age-old 'divide and conquer' plan.

The briefing officer went over the map routes and key landmarks like railroads, aerodromes, and roads for them to recognize from the air. He also explained where the I.P. (Initial Point) would be for them to start on their bombing run. Once they made it to that point, they had to stay on a straight course, without taking evasive action even in the face of intense flak. This was done in order to make a straight line for the target and to have an accurate bomb run. The Germans knew this and took full advantage of it with their anti-aircraft flak guns.

Reconnaissance photos were shown of the target area and where the aiming point would be, in this case at the center of the airfield. They were shown where the concentration of their bomb patterns should be in order to knock out the factory and airfield, along with some parked planes. Their bombing altitude was to be at 18,000 feet to ensure effective bombing results. This altitude was lower for better bombing accuracy, but it also made it more dangerous for them as they were easier targets for the German anti-aircraft batteries.

The airmen were briefed on how the other assembly forces (bomb divisions) would attack other targets and also provide a distraction to the Luftwaffe and lessen the attacks on their Combat Wing. They were reminded again of how crucial it was to destroy Gerry's air force both on the ground and in the air. The bombers and their crews were also the bait to allow our fighters to destroy the enemy's.

NUREMBERG A/D
49° 29' 00" N. 11° 05' 35" E.

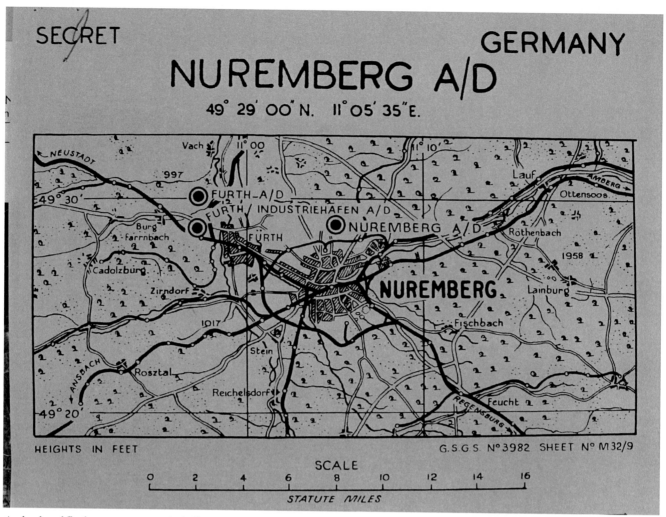

HEIGHTS IN FEET

G.S.G.S. N° 3982 SHEET N° M 32/9

SCALE

STATUTE MILES

A declassified secret target briefing map from the Strategic Bombing Survey folder at the National Archives, College Park, Maryland. The map shows both the Furth and Nuremberg Airdromes (A/D).

The crews were told by the flak officer that they would be flying over the Ruhr Valley in Germany, which was one of its most heavily defended areas due to the great concentration of industry there. It was the center of Germany's industrial might and war production. The bombers would be going over the heavily defended area on the way in, and on the way out. There would be hundreds of flak guns shooting at them from that region. The looks on the men's faces were somber to say the least. Some of the men thought for sure that the Air Force was trying to get rid of them and that they were going to die or get seriously hurt on this mission.

The weather officer described the weather patterns over both the British Isles and the Continent, which detailed the various places and altitudes. It was indicated that there would be 10/10 (solid) cloud cover with the cloud base at 1,000 over their airfield at their 9:30 AM take-off time. This would be a problem for forming the group, as the cloud tops could be anywhere from 25 feet to 3,000 feet high. Having other heavy bomber airfields within five to ten miles of each other could prove extremely hazardous in this kind of situation. Forming up each bomber group over its designated formation area could mean mid-air collisions as the planes lumbered to break through the cloud ceiling.

The good news was that the clouds would decrease rapidly over the English Channel and would be nil (clear) over the Continent. There would be a light haze over the target area. The flip side was that it would be -15°F (-26°C) at their bombing altitude. They were also briefed about the weather on their return route. Everything should be the same, only in reverse, except they were to expect 9-10/10 cloud cover over the Channel. When landing back at Tibenham, they would expect 8-10/10 cloud cover with the 1,000 foot ceiling remaining and the sporadic light rains over the base. Visibility below the cloud cover would be about five miles without the rain, and only two miles with the rain. This all meant that landing could be as dangerous as the take-off. Many crews cursed the weather over England.

The American aircrews already knew from their own experiences how accurate the enemy was getting with their anti-aircraft guns, as they had seen many of their fellow crews shot down over the Continent since the group flew its first mission. The entire group had already lost 25 crews and planes to date, out of the original 62 crews and planes that came over during November and December of 1943. One plane, from the 703rd squadron, was lost over the Caribbean on the way over when they most likely ditched in the sea due to a fuel transfer problem. There were no survivors. The rest were lost in combat on the 28 missions the group had flown since they started their combat operations. That amounted to a 41% loss in crews and planes in the first two and a half months of flying combat. The bomb group lost 13 of the 25 planes and crews on the infamous Gotha, Germany mission just the day before, on February 24th. On that mission 25 planes were sent out and only 12 came back. It was a 52% loss of men and planes in one day. At that rate, many of the men never expected to finish their 25-mission tour of duty. Despair set in when they were upped to 30 missions per man in mid-April. Of the surviving group's original flyers, many considered themselves already dead, as they were only about halfway through their missions. Crews typically were not to fly two days back-to-back, and missions were not every day, so the losses were spread out more over time. However, it didn't take a genius or a mathematician to figure out that one's number could be up soon. There were many empty or half-filled Nissen huts when the Gotha mission was over the day before. It was a grim reminder of the mortality rates the men were facing. Morale was dropping in the ranks quickly. Without fighter escorts that could make it all the way to the targets with them, many heavy bomber groups suffered such staggering losses. Although replacement crews would eventually arrive, seeing the empty cots on the other side of their huts made many an airman sick to his stomach, and in some cases terrified to fly anymore. Some didn't. Some men chose to give up their volunteer flight status and pay in order to work on the ground where it was safer.

Due to the heavy losses suffered the day before, and other mechanical difficulties, the group was only able to put up 17 planes for the mission. The Williams crew's original plane that they flew from the States to England, number 580, *"Hap"*

The author in front of a German Bf 110 night fighter at the Royal Air Force Museum in Hendon, England, on July 18, 2013.

445th Bomb Group Combat Crews and Planes Losses Between November 13, 1943 and February 25, 1944

There were 25 out of the original 62 planes and crews lost in that time.
That's 250 men lost (i.e. killed, captured, or MIA).
It was a 41% loss of the original group.
Many of the original crews were only halfway through their 25 missions.
The odds of survival of a tour of duty were less than 25%.

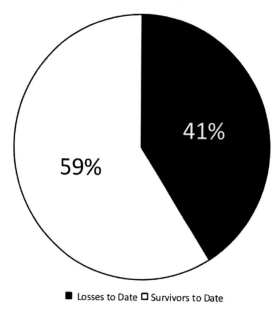

■ Losses to Date □ Survivors to Date

445th Bomb Group Combat Crews and Planes Losses on the Gotha, Germany raid on February 24, 1944 (the day before the raid on Nurnberg/Furth, Germany).

13 out of 25 crews and planes did not return to Tibenham Airfield.
That's 130 men who did not come back.
It was a 52% loss of the planes and crews dispatched that day.

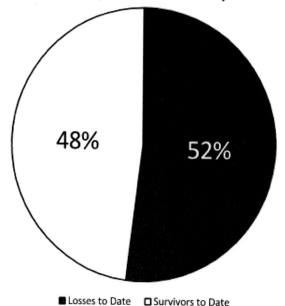

■ Losses to Date □ Survivors to Date

Hazard, was test flown at midnight to see if was ready for combat, but due to mechanical problems it stood down for the mission. Their squadron commander, Major James Stewart, would be flying in the lead plane, number 447 (name unknown), with Captain Neil Johnson's crew in the first flight element. The Williams crew would be his wingman to the left in number 118, *Nine Yanks and a Jerk*. 1st Lt. Bill Conley's crew would be flying as Stewart's right wingman, in the deputy lead position, in ship 132, *Tenovus* (the plane Stewart flew to England in when the group initially came to Tibenham back in November with 1st Lt. Sharrard's crew). Lt. George Wright's crew would be flying directly behind Stewart's plane in the 'slot' as the lead crew in the second flight in number 562, *Betty*. Both the Williams, Conley, and Wright crews would be flying in close formation in the lead element near Stewart's plane, where they could observe his flying and leadership skills, and he theirs.

Tail number 447 of the 703rd BS – the lead plane that day, with later tail markings. Photo – M. Simpson

Tenovus with its original pilots – at left, Lt. Lloyd Sharrard (pilot) and on the right, Lt. Chas. Wolfe (co-pilot). It was named as a play on words. Ten men to a crew ("ten of us") became *Tenovus*. On the Feb. 25, 1944 mission to bomb Nurnberg/Furth, Lt. Conley's crew flew in *Tenovus* to Stewart's right as Deputy Lead. Sharrard's crew stood down on this mission, which is why Conley's crew was flying their plane that day. Photo courtesy of John Sharrard.

Jimmy Stewart's Mortal Storm

In 1940, about a year before Stewart enlisted in the Air Corps, he made an anti-Nazi film called, *The Mortal Storm*. Even though Germany was never mentioned, its government took such offense to its implications regarding the cruelty and insidiousness character of the Nazi Party, that it banned all MGM films from Germany. Now that Stewart was flying combat missions over Nazi occupied Europe, capturing or killing Stewart would be a big propaganda ploy for the Nazis. Stewart was flying every mission that he could, and the most dangerous ones at that. Those in high command weren't too keen on it. They wanted to put the

A 1940 magazine ad for *The Mortal Storm*, an anti-Nazi propaganda film James Stewart had starred in a year before he entered the US Army Air Corps. It was somewhat of an omen.

reins on him, as they were afraid that he either might get killed, or be shot down and taken captive. Either way he would be used as propaganda by the Germans. Nevertheless, Stewart was determined to fly with his crews, and they were encouraged by his desire to fly with them. He quickly earned the respect of the men as they saw that he didn't use his Hollywood status to shirk his responsibilities. He was in the thick of it with them, and he was their leader in combat. He was unwavering about flying with his men. Stewart had literally earned his wings, and also the respect of all who knew him. Stewart's cool, calm, and collected leadership, while under fire, eased his crews' fears. Many of the men felt safer when he was leading their formation. Stewart's real-life role in the war paralleled some of his roles in his movies where his characters had to grapple with the challenges and dangers to life and limb, yet were met with a strong resolve.* In the movie *The Mortal Storm*, Stewart's character Martin Breitner stood up to and resisted the Nazi regime. Stewart and his men were now in their own 'mortal storm' as they faced the odds against their own mortality in the hostile skies over Nazi occupied Europe.

---

* Stewart himself later remarked, "If you think you might die at any moment you think more about the hereafter. I was really afraid of what the dawn might bring. Our group had suffered several casualties during the day and the next morning at dawn I was going to lead my squadron out again, deep into Germany. I got to imagining what might happen and I feared the worst. Fear is an insidious and deadly thing; it can warp judgment, freeze reflexes, breed mistakes, and worse, it's contagious. I could feel my own fear and knew that if it wasn't checked it could infect my crew members." He sought solace in his faith, and visited the base chapel often. "I guess it was because I kept being reminded that life can be short that I went to chapel regularly. During a scary moment in the skies, I would remember the 91st Psalm my father taught me." Stewart conquered his fear, and for his gallant leadership on a mission to Brunswick, was awarded the Distinguished Flying Cross. From the *Southern California 2nd Air Division Debriefing Team Newswire* newsletter, July/August 2004, p.26.

A 1940s magazine ad showing the dreaded ball turret. It was a rotating small sphere that contained twin .50 caliber machine guns and the gunner. The turret was lowered beneath the belly of the plane. Few airmen desired such a position. Hank Culver flew about 10 of his 30 combat missions inside this turret, as no one else wanted it. He would switch his position at the left waist gun with another gunner and get into the ball turret as needed.

The briefing officer that day said that the crews had to conserve as much fuel as they could. He cautioned them, "Don't drop your ball turret down into the slipstream unless you have to.[2] If you use it, get it back up inside the plane as quickly as you can. Open and close your bomb bay doors as quickly as possible. You have ten hours of fuel and nine and one half hours of flying time. There will be very little

2. It could decrease airspeed by ten miles per hour with the drag.

margin for deviating from the planned path of your flight." This would be the group's longest mission up to that date. The calculations for maximum gas loads and maximum bomb loads had been figured out in the most precise details.

Courtesy of www.lillinews.com

The officer continued, "Airplanes carrying K-20 cameras in their camera hatch, do not forget to turn them on. The tail gunner will do this" (Robinson, *A Reason to Live*, 1988, p.300). Six of the 17 planes would carry the K-20 (pictured at left), K-21, and K-24 types of cameras for photographing the bomb strikes from their high altitudes either through the open bomb bay doors or through a camera hatch on the floor near the radio operator.

Once the main briefing was over, the pilots, navigators, bombardiers, radio operators, and gunners each went to their own small briefings for further instructions. They went over their routes and timings. Flak batteries at various locations were reviewed. They also received their information folders, weather maps, charts, photographs, and other essential materials to ensure the success of the mission.

After their briefings, the crews went to the locker room to get their combat and flight gear on. It was the type of clothing and equipment designed to fend off another enemy, the biting sub-zero cold temperatures that they would encounter at high altitudes. The Williams crew dressed in the same locker room area as Major Stewart. Conversations and jokes were often exchanged between Stewart and his crews as they dressed for combat. (One later conversation would include a few words about this particular mission. Stewart would later remark to Frank Mangan in an earnest, yet assuring, tone, "When I see you, I wonder how in the Lord's name you are still alive.")

Stewart dressed the part like the rest of the men he served with. The airmen dressed as if they were going into an arctic zone. Each man climbed into his own 'Blue Bunny' - a powder blue colored, electrically heated flying suit, which went on over thermal underwear. After that, a heavy fleece-lined pair of leather flight pants went over the electric suit, followed by the similarly made B-3 bomber jacket. A yellow Mae West life preserver went on next, in case they had to ditch in the English Channel. The parachute harness was over that. Heavy fleece-lined leather gloves would go over both pairs of silk and wool gloves. The two outer gloves were more like mittens, but with a thumb and trigger finger for the gunners. Their heavy fleece-lined leather A-6 flying boots were put on over electric wool inserts, which were over heavy wool socks, which were over a pair of silk socks. A leather, fleece-lined B-5 flying helmet with built-in ear phones completed the headgear. The AN-6530 flight goggles were then strapped on over the helmet. An A-14 oxygen mask was the standard issue to be worn at altitudes above 10,000 feet. A flak vest and a flak helmet were usually put on when the plane was airborne and they were getting near the enemy coastline and flak batteries. Once on the plane, they would also wear a throat microphone snugly strapped around their necks to communicate with the rest of the crew.

All aircrew members received escape kits in case they were shot down over enemy territory. The kits provided maps, medical items, foreign currency and other essential items which could aid them in an escape back to Allied territory if needed. Co-pilot Douglas Pillow signed for the ten escape kits for this mission for the Williams crew. Henry Going signed for the parachute bags and K-rations (ex. dried food, gum, and chocolate), hoping that they wouldn't have to use them. The pilots, copilots, navigators, and bombardiers were issued battle folders containing important maps that would help them locate the target precisely, which they also signed for. All personal effects, like wallets, personal photographs,

Me in the gear that my father and his crew would've worn during their high altitude flights, in front of the Collings Foundation B-24J *Witchcraft* at Monmouth Executive Airport, Wall, New Jersey - August 2013.

The author in a summer flight suit with a replica USAAF flight bag and parachute in front of the Collings Foundation B-24J *Witchcraft* at Monmouth Executive Airport, Wall, New Jersey - August 2014.

(These two photos were taken a year apart.)

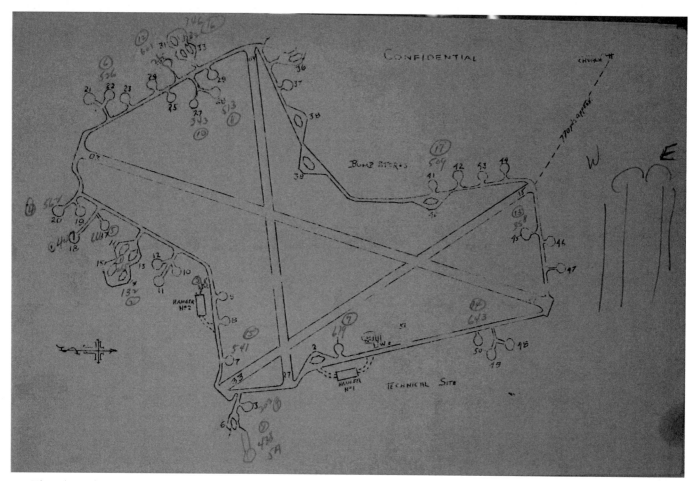

The aircraft hardstand/dispersal map at Tibenham Airfield, showing aircraft positions on February 25, 1944. Note aircraft positions penciled in. *NARA.*

An ordnance ground crew member arms the bombs on a B-24. *NARA*

and the like, had to be turned in, otherwise the articles might give the enemy too much information in case of capture.

Like their squadron commander, many an airman took comfort in his faith. Some of the crew members looked to their chaplains for prayers and blessings just prior to take-off. Sometimes a priest might place his hands upon each man's head and ask God to bless each one of the crew members so that they would return safely. As the saying goes, "There are no atheists in fox holes," so it was for many aircrews on heavy bombers. A lot of the men feared that the planes would become their coffins on any given mission. Among the many nicknames the B-24 was given, the "Flying Coffin" was one of them. The body of the plane looked like a huge coffin turned on its side, and sadly became the entombment for many airmen during the war. Asking for God's blessing was no sign of weakness to the crews. They knew that they were going to face death on each mission and were well aware of the mortality rates. They had seen many of their fellow airmen get shot down, or die from wounds received in combat in the previous days, weeks, and months. They would take all of the blessings they could get.

Once dressed, the Williams crew and another crew, got into a two and a half ton truck and were driven out to their assigned planes at their various hardstands at the dispersal areas. The many hardstands at Tibenham Airfield were buzzing with the aircrews and trucks and jeeps. Once there, the crews loaded their gear onto the bomb-laden planes as the aircraft squatted on the hardstands under the heavy weight of their loads. The ordnance personnel had already loaded the bombs and ammunition onto the plane. The bombs had been hoisted into the bomb bay racks to ensure that all would release from their racks with the greatest ease. Otherwise, a bomb that didn't release properly could jeopardize the entire mission for that crew and aircraft. The ground crews worked all night, having pre-flighted the plane, and were still putting on the finishing touches just prior to take-off. The ground crew chief, Master Sergeant Grant Murray, and his two assistants, had checked the entire plane over from the engines, props, wiring, wings, fuel system, gas tanks, oxygen system, communications system, bomb load, controls, having cleaned the plexiglass on the turrets and windows, and checked over a thousand other elements that make up a heavy bomber plane. The gas tanks were topped off at 2700 gallons of fuel. Every piece of the plane had to be in proper working order. At best, one malfunction could cause the plane to return to the base without

having reached its target. At worst, it could cause the plane some serious damage and the crew their lives.

The Williams crew, flying on *Nine Yanks and a Jerk,* was listed on the flight formation chart to be at hardstand 15 (see below), but was shown on the airfield hardstand map (above) to be on the apron next to the No. 2 T-hangar, both locations being on the southeast end of the airfield. Whichever site the plane was parked at, Technical Sergeant George Snook and Staff Sergeant Hank Culver, being the engineers, were to check over the exterior and interior of the plane for any signs of potential problems. George was also meticulous about making sure that the gas tanks were topped off. Even though M/Sgt. Murray would assure him that they were, George would reply back, "I'm the one flying in it... I'm checking it to be sure." They needed all the fuel they could carry for this mission. It was going to be a long haul and a long day. The two engineers and a couple of other enlisted men turned the propellers a full rotation by hand to

A ground crewman prepares a B-24 for combat by loading freshly filled oxygen bottles for the long mission ahead. The meticulous work of the ground crews was critical for the function and survival of the aircrews and for the success of the mission. They often worked throughout the night. *NARA.*

keep the oil from pooling in any one cylinder so that the engines would all have a good start. The pilot and co-pilot, Mack Williams and Douglas Pillow, also went around the plane, checking it over before getting into the cockpit.

Feeling a bit superstitious, some of the men suggested that they call this mission number "12B" instead of number "13." Mack pooh-poohed the idea, trying to reduce the anxiety of the men. Once the exterior checks were done, Mack called for everyone to get into their positions inside the plane. Once the men were in their positions, Mack ordered a throat microphone check to make sure that each man was in his position and could be heard by the others on the intercom. According to procedure, once in flight, Mack would order a microphone check about every ten minutes to make sure that each man was still breathing from his oxygen flow and that no one was in trouble. If a crew member failed to respond on the intercom, someone would be sent to check on the crewman to be sure he was okay.

Having gone through their pre-flight checklist, Mack and Doug started the engines on *Nine Yanks and a Jerk* at 9:20 AM. The rest of the crew got into their take-off positions. The group's 17 planes rolled out of their hardstand areas and on to the taxiway and got in line for takeoff. To personalize their planes, the crews had different names painted

DISPERSAL OF AIRCRAFT   DATE 24/2/44   1730 HOUR

DISPERSAL NO.	AIRCRAFT NO.	DISPERSAL NO.	AIRCRAFT NO.
1.	619 - N	26	601 - N
2	436 - T	27	343 - W
2A	532 - W	28	
3	201 - I	29	627 - I
4		30	
4A		31	
5		31A	
5A	438 - L	32	146 - P
6	306 - K	33	
6A	Oxford	33A	
7	541 - N	34	563 - P
8		35	
9	571 - D	35A	
10	652 (New A/C)	36	
11		37	126 - V
12		38	
13		38A	
14	132 - F	39	921 - W
14A	215 - DX	40	501 - R
15	118 - I	41	599,- T
16	580 - G	42	
16A		43	
17	666 - N	44	
18	447 - E	45	358 - U
19	319 - S (Hethel)	46	496 - K (Old Buckenham)
20	562 - O	47	
21		48	
22	526 - R	49	
24		50	643 - N
25		51	

HANGAR NO. 1   731-D   622-Z   602-J   348-H
HANGAR NO. 2   513-T   553-Q
RUNWAY

Signed *George E. Rowe*
(FOO on Duty)

2 Copies 1 - Operations
1 - Engineering

The aircraft dispersal list at Tibenham Airfield, showing aircraft positions at the hardstands on February 24, 1944, the night before.

on their planes like *Dixie Dudrop, Bunnie, Betty, Sin Ship, Ballsafire, Tenovus, Pistol Packin' Mama, Willer Run?, Sweatin It Out, Ramblin' Wreck, Available Jones,* and *Nita* to name a few. The taxiway passed right in front of the control tower. The lineup of warplanes was like a military parade in review. The roaring sound of the group's B-24 engines revved up and ready to tear into the morning air was deafening. The sounds of dozens of Pratt and Whitney engines and propellers reverberating through the quiet countryside was the sound of war waiting to be waged. The atmosphere around the base was filled with intensity, excitement, anticipation, and silent prayers as the once tranquil Norfolk County came alive with men and machines ready for combat. It was a dramatic sight and sound never to be forgotten by all who witnessed it. Even the ground shook. Many of the men who flew such missions remembered it decades later, as did the British men, women, and children who lived nearby.

At 9:30 AM, the green flare went up from the control tower officer's flare gun. It arched over the airfield in the early morning sky, signaling the crews that the mission was on.

B-24s lined up for take-off at Tibenham Airfield in England.
From the photo collection of Billy Fields via Jane (Fields) Deeds.

The control tower was abuzz with men watching from inside the glass house atop the control tower and those outside leaning against the ice cold railing as the battle ready planes took off in 30 to 45 second intervals. Many of the local Brits stopped their daily work or chores to see the heavy bombers take to the air, and offer up whispered prayers for the brave airmen. Farmers gave pause as they gazed at the sights of plane after plane slowly take-off to bring the war to the enemy across the Channel.

When it was his turn, Mack turned *Nine Yanks and a Jerk* onto the main runway, into the wind, and revved up the engines. Since the B-24's wheels had no steering, the pilots had to turn the planes by revving up one side's engines in order to turn the aircraft. The brakes squealed as the pilots positioned the bird for her long run down the runway. The plane rocked back and forth from nose to tail as the brakes were applied. With the brakes held tightly, the pilots tested the engines to check for any

Roland "Woody" Woods (Waist Gunner - standing far right) with Crew 71 in front of Dixie Dudrop of the 703rd Bomb Squadron on Feb. 24, 1944. They had just landed from the Gotha Mission. 25 Planes took off, and 13 were shot down. Twenty six German planes were claimed to have been shot down. The target was destroyed (a factory manufacturing Messerschmitt 109 fighters). A Presidential Unit Citation was awarded to 445th Bomb Group for this action. Photos here and next two pages from http://www.b24bestweb.com.

Photo contributor Ron Woods.

problems, making sure they were ready for a strenuous take off. The bomb bay doors were kept open to allow gas fumes to escape. The reason being that when the gas tanks were topped off for a long mission like this, it was likely that the raw gas might spill over and run down the sides of the bomb bay, where it would create fumes that could become dangerously explosive. One spark in such a situation would cause the plane to explode into a fireball. The Williams crew had seen it happen before – a pilot, co-pilot, or another crew member near the bomb bay on another plane may have either lit up a cigarette too soon during take-off, or some kind of random spark occurred, and a plane two places in front of them exploded on take-off. The fireball consumed the plane and its crew. The resultant explosion and concussion terrified the other crews. It was a tragedy that left them shaken up more than once. For these reasons the bomb bay doors would be closed last. Once they were sufficiently airborne and had switched over to the main tanks from the reserves, then those who smoked could light up.

445TH BOMB GROUP NOSE ART

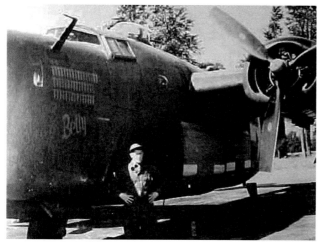

Betty from the 703rd Bomb Squadron.   *Available Jones* from the 701st Bomb Squadron.

The 700th Bomb Squadron's B-24 *Bunnie*.

Photo contributors -Top: (r) Pete Johnston; (l): Ivo DeJong, Bottom: C.M. Lawson

Mack and Doug went through their final checklist. With the engines performing well, they cranked them up to take-off speed, released the brakes, and the burdened plane roared down the runway. With such a heavy bomb load, Mack used most of the 6,000 foot long runway to ease the ship into the air. The rest of the crew remained in their take-off positions, listening to the familiar drone of the engines as the propellers cut through the cold, wet air to get the ship aloft. There was always an excitement in experiencing a heavy bomber gaining speed down the runway, no matter how many times an airman did it. The hum and drone of the engines, the vibrations throughout the plane, and the sight of

Weepin Willy from the 702nd Bomb Squadron.

Photo contributor Brendan Wood

Sweatin It Out from the 700th BS

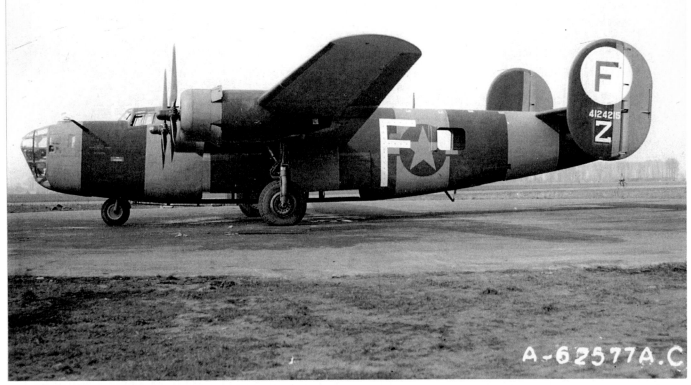

Above. The 445th Bomb Group's formation ship, ***Lucky Gordon***, also referred to as the "zebra ship" by the men stationed at the base. It was a war weary B-24D model turned into an assembly ship. Its high visibility black and orange stripes made it easy for the pilots to see as they formed up on this plane's lead in flight during group assemblies. Photo from *NARA*. Mack Williams, Douglas Pillow, George Snook, Frank Mangan, and Billy Fields had flown in this plane at various times when they were not flying combat missions.

the ground getting further away as the bird lifted off the ground made one feel that he was part of something greater than himself. Adrenaline rushed through their veins as the plane gained speed down the runway and climbed into the air. The feeling of exhilaration pulsed through their bodies as the sound of the four Pratt and Whitney engines reverberated throughout the plane and the propellers chopped and beat at the air around them. The men and their machines were fully awake and in action now.

It was 9:33 AM when they left Tibenham. The pilots would have to get above the 1,000 foot cloud ceiling in order to be able to have clear visibility and form up with the rest of the group. The visibility at take-off was about five miles, with a haze. The cloud tops varied from 25 feet to 3,000 feet, as briefed.

The group assembly took a little longer due to the overcast skies over the base. The solid cloud cover over Tibenham was a precarious situation. With other airfields just five to ten miles away from each other, other groups were forming their flight elements at the same time. It was always a nerve-racking experience to form a group in such crowded airspace over Norfolk County. It would take the group a total of four and a half hours to assemble their group, form with other groups, and fly to the target. They did all of this without modern-day radar. It was always an amazing feat of piloting skills.

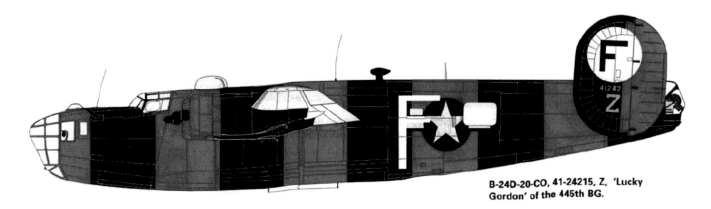

B-24D-20-CO, 41-24215, Z, 'Lucky Gordon' of the 445th BG.

Above: A color version of **Lucky Gordon** from *SAM - Scale Aircraft Modelling Magazine*, Vol.21, No.6, August 1999; Published by Guideline Publications and printed by Regal Litho Ltd. Courtesy of Regis Auckland. Below: An example of a group forming on its assembly ship - the 458th BG's **Spotted Ass Ape**, in the lead with the group in trail. Colorful, audacious names were often given to the assembly planes to help personalize them. This is how bomber formations assembled over the North Sea for combat missions to bring their payloads to Germany. During World War II, dozens of group formations like these were seen on a regular basis by the local Brits on the ground and by the Americans on their air bases across Norfolk and Suffolk counties in Britain. Many a U.S. airman had these iconic views forever etched into his memory as part of his wartime experiences. The planes below have the later, colorful high visibility tail markings. *NARA*

Above: B-24s over East Anglia in England. It would take a few hours to assemble a group, a combat wing, and the whole 2nd Air Division. The 2nd Air Division B-24s would then meet up with the 1st and 3rd Air Divisions of B-17s on their way to bomb their targets on the Continent. From USAF at http://www.globalaviationresource.com/v2/2014/02/20/d-day-70-pt-3-operation-argument-the-big-week-bomber-offensive-february-1944/. Below: A 445BG B-24, *Conquest Cavalier*, with early markings. *NARA*

By 10:20 AM the 445th Bomb Group's formation was complete, except for one crew that couldn't find the formation. In number 526, 1st Lt. Pavelka's crew flying **Willer Run?** from the 702nd Squadron, couldn't find the formation when the group initially formed near the base, and had to return to the airfield. In spite of that, the rest of the crews had all formed on their black and orange-striped formation ship called **Lucky Gordon**, also known to the crews as the "zebra ship," which was out in front, just ahead of the group. The comical looking plane was easily seen from a distance because of its intentional, high visibility paint scheme, as it circled around the invisible *Buncher 6* radio beacon, waiting for the group to form on its lead. Red flares were fired from **Lucky Gordon** to help the assembling planes find their formation. It took just under an hour to get the group in its own formation above the cloud cover before forming up with the other groups in their Combat Wings.

First, the three bomb groups in the Second Combat Wing had to form together – the 445th from Tibenham, the 389th from Hethel, and the 453rd from Old Buckenham. At 10:26 AM, the 445th formed on the 389th, high and to their right, followed by the 453rd, which formed on the 389th, high and to their left. The three groups formed very well over the *Buncher 6* radio beacon at Hethel at the 8,000 foot level, except the 453rd didn't have its formation completed yet. The radio beacon allowed them to form together at the appropriate distances without colliding with each other. There was always a major risk of mid-air collisions involved during overcast days. In spite of the 453rd's delay, the 2nd Combat Wing still departed from their designated assembly area on time.

A group of B-24s from the 458th Bomb Group assemble over the East Anglian countryside, with the North Sea in the background. This photo illustrates later high visibility tail markings assigned to B-24s. The airspace over rural England was incredibly crowded as groups, wings, and the 2nd Air Division assembled for a mission. *NARA*

445th Bomb Group Formation Chart for Positions at Group Assembly
FINAL *BIG WEEK* MISSION: Mission to Nurnberg, Germany – Friday, February 25, 1944

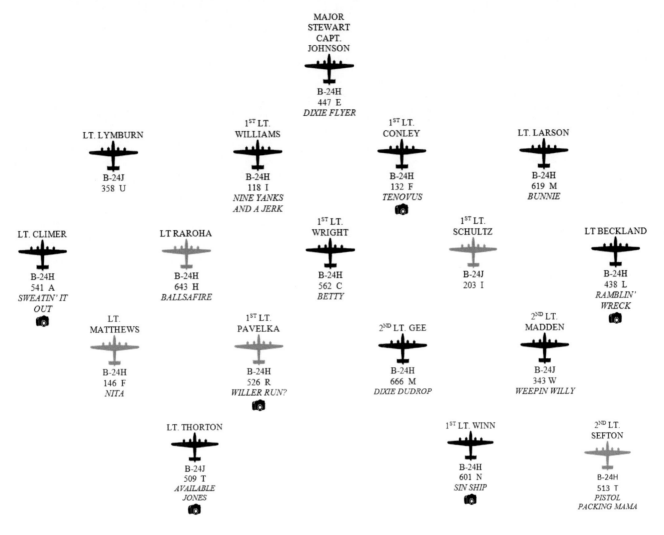

MAJOR
STEWART
CAPT.
JOHNSON
B-24H
447 E
DIXIE FLYER

LT. LYMBURN
B-24J
358 U

1ST LT.
WILLIAMS
B-24H
118 I
*NINE YANKS
AND A JERK*

1ST LT.
CONLEY
B-24H
132 F
TENOVUS

LT. LARSON
B-24H
619 M
BUNNIE

LT. CLIMER
B-24H
541 A
*SWEATIN' IT
OUT*

LT RAROHA
B-24H
643 H
BALLSAFIRE

1ST LT.
WRIGHT
B-24H
562 C
BETTY

1ST LT.
SCHULTZ
B-24J
203 I

LT BECKLAND
B-24H
438 L
*RAMBLIN'
WRECK*

LT.
MATTHEWS
B-24H
146 F
NITA

1ST LT.
PAVELKA
B-24H
526 R
WILLER RUN?

2ND LT. GEE
B-24H
666 M
DIXIE DUDROP

2ND LT.
MADDEN
B-24J
343 W
WEEPIN WILLY

LT. THORTON
B-24J
509 T
*AVAILABLE
JONES*

1ST LT. WINN
B-24H
601 N
SIN SHIP

2ND LT.
SEFTON
B-24H
513 T
*PISTOL
PACKING MAMA*

Symbols and Descriptions Key

	PLANES DISPATCHED AND OVER TARGET		PLANES DISPATCHED BUT NOT OVER TARGET DUE TO ENEMY ACTION, EQUIPMENT FAILURE, OR HUMAN ERROR	PILOT'S NAME AND RANK IF KNOWN TYPE OF AIRCRAFT AND MODEL · SERIAL NUMBER AND CALL LETTER ON TAIL NAME OF PLANE IF KNOWN	K-20, K-21, OR K-24 CAMERAS CARRIED ON BOARD TO PHOTOGRAPH BOMB STRIKES

Two different B-24 nose turrets: the A15 Emerson Turret found on late J and H models, and the A6B Consolidated Turret.

A 445th Bomb Group B-24 formation over France. Photo courtesy of Jane (Fields) Deeds).

The blue waters of the English Channel and the English coastline just west of Dungeness. This is the same view my father's crew saw as they left England to head toward the French coast just across the English Channel. Photo taken by the author as he was on a flight from Edinburgh, Scotland to Paris, France on July 3, 2014. We followed a similar flight pattern.

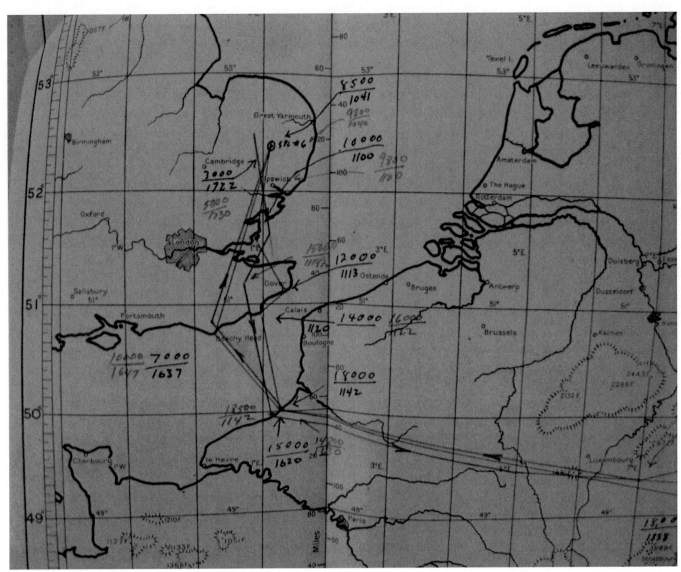

Part of the flight route map from the 445th Bomb Group's mission folder for the February 25, 1944 mission to Nurnberg, Germany. It shows the routes in and out, planned and actual ones. *NARA*.

The Wing then flew south past Great Yarmouth and formed up with other Second Air Division Combat Wings over the *Splasher 6* radio beacon to the Second Air Division's assembly area. As they approached the 10,000 foot altitude mark the crews were told to put on their oxygen masks and check the oxygen tanks and levels. It was U.S. Army Air Force regulations that any flights over that altitude required the crews to be on oxygen. Several minutes without oxygen at those altitudes at first would leave an airman severely disoriented, then he would pass out, and within ten to fifteen minutes without oxygen he would be dead. Mack called for each man to reply back from his position every ten minutes.

The formation was eighteen miles northwest of Ipswich at 10:43 AM, and then headed over the area where the Thames River meets the North Sea. If it had been a clear day, London could've been seen from a distance on the right side of the planes. The Second Combat Wing got in place behind the Twentieth Combat Wing and proceeded south toward Dover, England. Once they were over Dover at 11:13 AM, they headed southwest over the English Channel, staying close to the English coastline. Between 10:43 and 11:19 AM, they had gained 7,000 feet in altitude from 8,500 to 15,500 feet. Watching England disappear behind them was always a foreboding feeling. It left many an airman wondering if he would ever see the island nation, his temporary home, again.

At 11:22 AM, the Second Combat Wing crossed the English coast at Dungeness, a minute and a half later than their briefed time, and made a sharp left turn to head south over the Channel. Once over the Channel, the gunners were given the order to test fire their guns to make sure they were in proper working order. Within 20 minutes they would be over the enemy coast and had to be ready for possible immediate attacks from enemy fighters. Now was the time to check for jammed guns or any other problems. The gunners were told to oil their guns well, but not too much to avoid freezing higher up.

After flying almost directly south over the Channel, they made up some time and made landfall at 11:42 AM at a point just two miles north of Dieppe, a beautiful port city in northern France. The clouds had cleared over the Channel and over the Continent, just like the weather officer had mentioned. The serene light blue waters of the French coastline were picturesque, almost tranquilizing as they reflected the midday sunlight. The 445th Bomb Group had just obtained their correct altitude with everything being routine until they arrived over the enemy coast, where the resort-like scene was disrupted by the reality of war. It was over this area where Major Stewart's plane was suddenly hit with an accurate first burst of flak at 18,500 feet. Stewart later said in the mission report, "… we got a short burst of flak sent up by some real sharp shooters." The burst shot out his navigator's, 1st Lt. Howard Sellke's, Gee Box

(radio navigation system) and radio compass, and did some minor damage to 447. Thankfully no one was hurt, but the crew was a bit shaken up. It was a rude wake-up call from an enemy who let them know that they were not welcome. France was still very much occupied by the Germans, and they let the American bombers know it. It was critical that the bombers take evasive action from the flak batteries along the route ahead. Stewart calmly continued to lead the group a little south of their course and had to do some "S" turns to avoid enemy flak. The group was able to make

Rural areas in northern France today have not changed much since WWII. They still look like beautiful patchwork quilts as in this July 2013 photo taken over a section of northern France on an approach to Paris. The crews saw a lot of this on the way to the target, only in the dead of winter.

up the time by increasing their airspeed a little and with an unexpected wind decrease, thankfully. Their cruising speed was between 165-168 mph. This helped to conserve on fuel and to keep them on track with their briefed time as much as possible.

Hank Culver, flying in the left waist gun position of *Nine Yanks and a Jerk*, was prone to air and motion sickness on just about every mission. Because of the evasive maneuvers, he kept a brown, paper barf bag near him on every mission in case he got sick. With all of the "S" turning to avoid flak, the turbulence, and the plane's bobbing up and down like a cork in the ocean, Culver wound up giving his breakfast back into the bag, which he threw out over enemy territory as a specialty 'bomb' for the Germans. It had become a routine ritual for the wiry 20 year old waist gunner. At six feet tall and 160 pounds, Culver couldn't afford losing his breakfast on these missions. Like all airmen, he needed all of the energy and strength he could muster for combat. Nevertheless, somewhere down below came a surprise package from 18,000 feet high - 'bombs away!' Here's one for Hitler, and for Goring too!

At 12:25 PM, the Williams crew noted (as later recorded in their debriefing sheet) that they saw four to six enemy flak guns shooting at them about four miles east of Orly, France. As long as the shells were at a distance where they couldn't be heard, the crews were relatively safe. Once the exploding shells were close enough to be heard, as well as seen and smelled (because the cordite in the shells had a distinctive odor) they were something to be concerned about. There was nowhere to hide in the sky. The steel splinters from the shrapnel could take out a man's eye, or pierce his heart. Sometimes gunners would place flak vests on the floor so that they wouldn't get hit with shrapnel from below. The planes and their crews felt like sitting ducks in the air. They couldn't shoot back at flak. Around 12:32 PM, they experienced more flak from an area near Rethel, France. Stewart noted in the mission report that the enemy flak was "Moderate and accurate along [the] course from [the] enemy coast to Rhine River." He also noted that the friendly fighter protection was "Excellent on way in as far as Ludwigshaven – nil from there on and nil over target." Fortunately, few enemy fighters had been seen up to that point.

The first half of the mission was quite a diverse aerial tour - five countries in three hours - southeast England, northern and eastern France, Belgium, Luxembourg and then deep into central Germany. As the group flew over Europe, below them were hundreds of miles of beautiful farmland and forests. From their high altitude it looked like a patchwork quilt, with occasional villages and cities scattered throughout. Apart from the war, it looked like a peaceful, still painting they were flying over.

The occasional bursts of moderate and accurate flak shot at them along the way reminded them that they were not on a scenic tour, but were entering deadly airspace. There were angry guns below them amidst the scenic countryside carpeting. The formation of B-24s on the way to their target had to avoid city areas, railroad yards, and airfields, because that is where the most flak batteries typically were, not to mention fighters.

The calm scenery was once again interrupted with more fireworks than they cared to experience.

Aircraft 41-29146, **Nita**, of the 701st Squadron, 445th Bomb Group with the later high visibility tail markings that were applied in April of 1944. From website http://www.b24bestweb.com/nita-v1.htm
Contributor Tom Brittan

1st Lt. Jesse Cummings, the navigator on the Williams crew, kept meticulous notes on his navigator's log chart as to what was happening along the way. He kept busy throughout the flight noting their location at various times and places, keeping track of flak bursts, flak batteries, enemy installations such as airfields, and railroad marshalling yards. He noted, a half an hour later, as they crossed the German border, how they got a few bursts of flak near Saarbrucken, Germany as the Combat Wing was slightly off course. At 1:28 PM, they flew over the Rhine River just south of Germersheim where the enemy shot about 10-12 more bursts of flak at them. No one suffered much damage yet, except one plane. Aircraft number 203 from the 445th Bomb Group's 700th Bomb Squadron, Lt. Schultz's crew, had to leave the formation because the oil line in their number two engine was punctured by flak, and the top turret plexiglass was shattered due to flak. Even though they didn't make it over the target area, they were given credit for the mission because they encountered enemy action from the flak bursts. In addition, four other planes that were dispatched and had not encountered enemy action or made it over the target area due to various problems had received no sortie credit for having to abort the mission. Those crews were as follows– 1st Lt. Pavelka's crew, which flew in number 526, **Willer Run?**, of the 702nd Squadron, as mentioned earlier, couldn't find the formation when the group initially formed up

Aircraft 42-7513, **Pistol Packin' Mama**, of the 702nd Squadron, 445th Bomb Group with the early markings of the bomb group prior to the newer, high visibility tail markings that would be applied in April of 1944. From website http://www.b24bestweb.com/pistolpackinmama-v12.htm.

over England. Number 146, **Nita**, of the 701st Squadron, with Lt. Matthews' crew, had left the formation due to an oil leak and a manifold mercury fluctuation, both in the number three engine. Aircraft 513, **Pistol Packin' Mama**, of the 702nd Squadron, with 2nd Lt. Sefton's crew, left the formation as they reported that their interphones were inoperative due to a short circuit in an interphone connection.

Lt. Raroha's crew of the 700th Squadron, flying in number 643, **Ballsafire**, departed from the formation because they reported that their number two engine and the tail and upper turrets were inoperative, and that they also had a leak in their oxygen system. As a result, only twelve of the seventeen planes sent out from Tibenham would attack the target. It was disheartening to the other crews to see parts of their formation depart. Their collective firepower against enemy fighter attacks was thus diminished. Not to mention that there would be fewer bombs on the target.

The formation surprisingly encountered little enemy fighter resistance on the way in. About 15 black and white striped German Me 109s (see p.108) attempted attacks from the rear and below their group, that is, until the ball turrets were lowered, which warded them off. Friendly fighter protection was poor after Ludwigshaven. They had flown one segment of the mission over enemy territory for one hour and forty-five minutes without any Allied fighter escorts. 1st Lt. Williams' radio operator on **Nine Yanks and a Jerk**, T/Sgt. Frank Mangan, guarded the VHF Channel "C" on their radio in order to keep in contact with American fighter planes in case they had to call for help. Once over the target, only four American P-38 fighter escorts were seen protecting the formations. The post-mission critique would see a suggestion written down asking for all crews to be allowed access to the "C" Channel in order to call for friendly fighter protection, "especially in these big raids where the [American] fighters have a lot of coverage." More than one crew felt the same way. Other suggestions also made it into the mission critique. Airmen on the various crews also wanted back-fitting parachutes, instead of the bottom fitting ones on their seats, for easier maneuverability and a quick bailout if necessary. Some also wanted spare oxygen masks on their planes in case of emergencies should a mask or hose freeze up or if one were damaged due to enemy fire or shrapnel from flak bursts. What the enemy didn't finish, the high altitude, sub-zero temperatures and lack of oxygen would. Many crews learned this the hard way.[4]

At 1:59 PM, the group made it to the Combat Wing's I.P. (Initial Point, i.e. where they would turn onto the course designated for their approach to the bomb run) nine to ten minutes ahead of schedule. At 2:08 PM, they made it to their Group I.P., where they had to fly straight on course to the target, without any evasive action being allowed. They picked up the target from 20 miles away, and made a good, long bomb run. Stewart's bombardier, 1st Lt. William Robinson, sighted the target for range and course, while the deputy lead bombardier, 1st Lt. Daniel, on Conley's plane also sighted for range. The group's formation was good, with the second element trailing a little, but with good lateral distance as they headed toward the target. Some of the crews were a little confused about some of the call signals to be

Hank Culver's left waist gun position viewed from outside the Collings Foundation's B-24 Liberator *Witchcraft* on August 21, 2014. His 'son of a gunner' (the author) is at the .50 caliber gun.

used, and mentioned that in their post-mission debriefings and critiques. At the Group I.P. the signal flares were fired for the bombers to open their bomb bay doors.

A rush of freezing wind came through the open bombers which exposed the men in the waist gun positions even more to the frigid outside air. The temperature outside was -30°F (-35°C). The waist gunners experienced it the most, as it felt like a wind tunnel coming through their positions right behind the open bomb bay. The target was easily identified from smoke and explosions from previous bombs dropped by the other Combat Wings ahead of them. The 389th BG made the turn at the I.P. a little slowly, and so the 445th was forced to bomb ahead of them. At 2:11 PM, while flying at 18,000 feet in altitude, the William's crew, along with the rest of their group and Combat Wing, unloaded their bomb load on the designated aircraft repair factory and airfield. When the lead bombardier's bombs were

---

4. My father would come to know it very personally on a later mission to Berlin on April 29, 1944, when his oxygen mask and hose froze up and he passed out from lack of oxygen. Thankfully, his fellow waist gunner, Billy Fields, happened to have a spare oxygen mask that day. Fields saved his life with it. My father also had gotten frostbite while on his second mission, the one to Bremen, Germany on December 20, 1943. His fingers were very sensitive to cold after that, even decades after the war.

released, the rest of the group unloaded on his cue. The bombing was done visually, as it was clear weather over the target area, just as predicted. Their aiming point was right in the center of the airfield at Furth, as briefed.

On the Williams crew, 1ˢᵗ Lt. Jack Heany watched for the cue from the lead bombardier. As Jack saw the released bombs of the lead bombardier's plane drop, he pulled the toggle switch that released *Nine Yanks and a Jerk's* forty M1 Fragmentation Cluster bombs with their instantaneous fuses. Jack watched the bomb strikes through the windows of his nose compartment and the famous top secret Norden Bomb Sight. He and Jesse Cummings made notes of the time and the accuracy of the strikes. Stewart's navigator, Sellke, also noted how he had watched the bombs from the lead sections of both groups hit the airfield below with excellent results. Stewart's radio operator, Tech. Sergeant Buchman, radioed the bomb strike message to headquarters, noting it went very well. The bomb run lasted about four minutes. The planes immediately rose upward as the weight of the bombs left the ships. The pilots then quickly nosed the planes downward. Right after Jack Heany released the bombs from *Nine Yanks and a Jerk*, he closed the bomb bay doors. Then Mack, along with co-pilot Douglas Pillow, following

My father's left waist gun position on a B-24. I'm holding a .50 caliber machine gun like the one my father fired from this position on many of his missions. I'm wearing a summer flight suit, as it was over 90°F (32°C). Photo taken on August 21, 2014, inside the Collings Foundation's B-24 Liberator *Witchcraft*.

'BOMBS AWAY!'

From top left to bottom right. The above photos illustrate how the lead bombardier Lt. Sellke (and the others who followed, like Lt. Jack Heany and other bombardiers) got their bombs on the target. **1**) The bombardier (i.e. the bomb aimer) calculated the bombs' trajectory as he calibrated the famous top secret Norden bombsight. He checked for airspeed, wind drift, and aimed the crosshairs over the target. **2**) As they approached the target, he opened the electric bomb bay doors. **3**) While he flew the plane over the target, he called out "Bombs Away!" as he pressed the toggle switch on the bomb release mechanism. **4**) As the bombs fell on the target he continued to monitor their hits for accuracy and report what he saw. **5**) It became standard practice for an entire group of B-24s to drop their bombs as they saw the lead bombardier drop his. **6**) K20s and other cameras were used to photograph the bomb strikes for later analysis. Stills are from *NARA* and the famous WWII documentary *Target for Today* (1944), which was filmed in late 1943 and 1944 at various bomber bases in England and over the targets in Europe. Jimmy Stewart, the Williams crew, and the rest of their group lived through (in like manner) the planning, execution, and analysis of many such strategic bombing missions.

TARGET MAPS

Maps such as the above example were used by pilots, navigators, and bombardiers to pinpoint the targets they were to bomb. The purple, gray, and black colors were used to differentiate the target areas from non-strategic areas. The colors also showed up under black light in case they had to fly night missions and use black lighting inside the plane. This was done to avoid detection from enemy fighters who might see their lights. *NARA*

Stewart's lead, took the plane down about 500 feet in altitude according to standard mission procedure. This was done in order to throw off the enemy flak gunners and to gain enough air speed to quickly escape from the target area. The crews watched as the target was seen to be ablaze, and five of the enemy's parked planes on the airfield below exploded.

THE UNEXPLODED SHELL'S IMPACT

As *Nine Yanks and a Jerk* was halfway through a sharp, banking left turn to head back to England, the German flak gunners tracked their formation and filled the air around them with exploding shells. The flak was moderate to heavy, and accurate. The black puffs of smoke rained down and shot upwards, steel splinters into the warbird's skin. Streams of daylight appeared through parts of their plane as shrapnel punched new holes through the plane's thin hull. As time seemed to stand still, the amount of holes rapidly increased. There was nothing to do to stop them. Then suddenly – BANG! The plane shuddered. One .88mm anti-aircraft shell ripped through their plane, without exploding. It rocked the ship. The screeching shell went through the bomb bay, tore out part of the catwalk, and just missed the radio operator Frank Mangan by about two feet, tearing away part of the floor near him. It went through an instrument box, shredded a radio set, and then tore the half-inch armor plating off the back of the pilot Mack Williams' seat, just missing him by inches. The screaming sound of the shell and the tearing of

The bomb bay catwalk looking toward the front of the plane. The yellow arrow shows the path and concussion of the shell. The .88mm shell tore out the front part of the catwalk just before the radio operator's compartment. Thankfully it was after the bombs had been dropped. This is a still frame taken from the author's video camera on a flight in the Collings Foundation B-24J *Witchcraft* on August 24, 2013. Notice the dummy bomb on the left with the yellow stripe painted on it. The catwalk is less than ten inches wide. The bomb bay doors are thin aluminum and would not hold the weight of a man. We were warned not to step onto the bomb doors while in flight, as the doors would collapse under our feet.

Above: An artist's depiction of the moment of impact when the .88mm shell tore through *Nine Yanks and a Jerk*. The print is based on eyewitness accounts and the official mission papers from the U.S. Army Air Force folders of the 445th Bomb Group held at the National Archives. The shell entered the plane through the bomb bay and exited out the side behind the pilot. The dark orange arrow shows the path of the debris that was sucked out the hole in the shell's wake, where it went over the wing and ripped the .50 caliber machine gun out of Hank Culver's hands as he was firing at an enemy plane. Below: A closer look at the shell's exit, the new hole the size of a window, and the flying debris that hit Culver's gun. Painting by Jason Breidenbach.

metal frightened the crew. They were flying through the heaviest flak barrage they had seen until that time. The shells were supposed to explode at certain altitudes or upon impact, but thankfully this one didn't. It was a dud! Even so, it was terrifying.

The exiting shell took the top turret gunner's, George Snook, packed parachute and unshod combat boots off the flight deck and right out the hole big enough for a man's head to fit through. The plane's side was marred by the jagged hole the shell had made. The once smooth skin of the Liberator was fanned outward with jagged metal edges flailing in the slipstream. Aluminum flakes scattered on the flight deck. It also blew the radio operator Frank Mangan's packed parachute out the hole. All that was left on the flight deck of Frank's parachute was the red handle to pull the rip cord with, which he kept as a souvenir after the war. The rest of the chute went out the hole. Another chute

The inside of a B-24 Liberator as seen through an open bomb bay door. The whizzing shell followed the path the arrow indicates. It took out part of the bomb bay catwalk, just missed Frank Mangan the radio operator (shown above in a life-size model) and the top turret gunner, George Snook (whose position is just out of view to the left and above the radio operator. The plexiglass is only for display at the museum. It is not original to a Liberator's design. Photo taken by the author on the B-24 Liberator at the Pima Air Museum in Tucson Arizona in April of 2015.

popped open on the flight deck, which added more chaos to the moment. The boots and packed parachutes had been on the flight deck right behind Mack's seat, behind the armor plating that was protecting him.

The debris from the packed parachutes and boots went out the hole, and the slip stream whisked the pieces past the left waist gun position where Hank Culver was and knocked the .50 caliber machine gun right out of his hands while he was firing at an enemy aircraft. The gun remained on its swivel post, but the debris also took the gun sight right off of the end of the gun barrel he was firing. Culver was startled because he didn't know what it was that just went by. Hank explained the story,

We got hit by anti-aircraft fire... it took out our hydraulic system. And behind the pilot there's a half-inch armor plating that protects him. It [the .88mm shell] took the armor plating off, from behind the pilot. It didn't explode. It just went through the ship, and the debris from the flight deck went back (and I was at the waist gun that day firing at an enemy) and it took the post sight right off of my gun and took the machine gun right out of my hands.

Some of the crew on the plane behind them, *Betty* (flown by Lt. Wright's crew), saw all of this happen, and watched as a packed parachute bounced off their number one engine propeller. Wright's plane dropped a little lower in altitude to see the large hole that was made underneath the damaged bomber. It was quite a hole underneath. The inside of the plane became colder with the added draft from the shell holes both beneath the plane and on its side. George, the flight engineer, remarked years later in an interview with the author, that if the shell had not been a dud, they would've been blown to smithereens:

> *I'm up in the top turret, and he [Frank] is on my immediate right, at his [radio] desk, and that shell coming up underneath me, and pretty damn close to him, and hitting the armor plating behind the pilot... was close.*
>
> *When that shell hit that armor [plating] behind the pilot, it took that great big hunk of steel and pushed it right down in the bomb bay. I don't remember whether it took the bomb bay out, or whether we opened the bomb bay and dropped it. The bombs were gone. There were no bombs aboard. It also took my packed parachute and boots right out the hole!*
>
> *I always say, thank God it was made by slave labor and it didn't go off. Fortunately it was built by slave labor and it was a dud. Had it been live ... we would've been blown sky high in a minute, which I've seen happen numerous times over my period of time serving overseas.*

Even though it was a dud, if the shell had hit one of the wings, it would've erupted the fuel tanks and set the plane in an unrecoverable downward spiral. A few more feet to the left or right and the wing tanks would've exploded thus causing the wings to fold. The plane would've gone down in pieces without a chance for any of the crew to escape.

The men were so busy doing their jobs, they didn't have time to think through all of the possible outcomes until later. Billy Fields had a few words to say right after the mission - *"It was a good thing that shell was a dud or somebody might have been hurt."* Frank Mangan wrote in his diary that night, *"One terrible mission way in Germany to Nurnberg. No fighters. [An] .88mm shell missed me. Tore floor up and side of ship. Blew my chute out. Only the Lord saved us that day."* Frank later wrote to his parents in Binghamton, New York,

> *We took our longest one into Germany yet and just after bombs away a flak shell came through the bottom of the plane, through the floor of the flight deck about two feet from my feet and it went into an instrument box and tore the side of the plane out.*

Frank said in his diary that his chute was blown out of the hole, while George said that his was blown out of the hole. It appears both went out the hole, while another one was damaged and popped-open on the flight deck.

The navigator, Jesse Cummings, was alarmed by the impact. He explained it many years later,

> *Heany was working on the bomb sight and summing up, ready to go... and all of a sudden – WHAM! The noise, and the smell of cordite, and the airplane guns. And it wasn't ten seconds that I realized what it was. But, I mean I just knew we'd been hit with an exploding .88mm. The smell, the lurch, the noise. I was so frightened in that moment, that even though I returned to my senses... knew what it was... I had to take my left hand, reach over and take my right hand and make it pick up my pencil to write down the target*

time. I'm not kidding. By the time I wrote that up I'm laughing to my silly self. But that's what happens when you're paralyzed. I couldn't make my right arm do what it's supposed to. And, now, that's fear.

The tail gunner, Joe Minton recorded the event decades later in his unpublished booklet, *Ten Men and a Bomber* (1992):

What damage the enemy fighters failed to do, the usual amount of flak along the route caused some concern. Flying alongside another aircraft, a ground shell neatly clipped off a propeller. It continued to fly on three propellers. About the same time another shell came up through our aircraft in the area [right behind] the pilot.

The shell didn't explode but went clear through the flight deck taking an extra parachute with it. No one was hurt, but slightly scared. The bombs had already gone to the ground. Everyone looked around. The engines continued to purr as if nothing happened. The intercom system had been knocked out so nobody could communicate with each other.

When it was possible, a check was made of the damage. The shell had severed the main hydraulic line under the flight deck, splintered a radio set, tore the thick armor plating from its moorings [from behind the pilot's seat], and damaged another parachute.

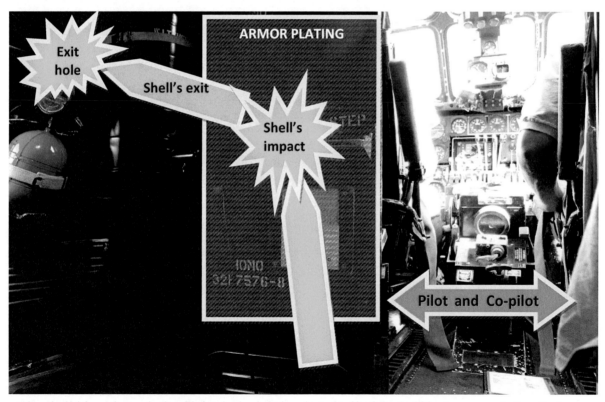

The shell blew through the flight deck and ricocheted off of the half-inch armor plating that was behind the pilot's seat and ripped it off of its moorings. The armor plating would've been where the green panel is behind the pilot. The half-inch armor was there to protect the pilot, which is exactly what it did – it saved Mack's life. The shell then blew a hole the size of a window as it exited the plane, taking George's unshod combat boots, and his and Frank's packed parachutes out of the hole. Photo taken on board the Collings Foundation's B-24J Liberator on August 24, 2013.

The trip back to Tibenham was uneventful. No one said much, partly because what had happened earlier. The danger was not over. With no hydraulic fluid, there was the danger of crashing when an attempt was made to land.

With part of its communications and hydraulics systems shot out by the .88mm shell, **Nine Yanks and a Jerk** had to make the arduous three hour and thirty-four minute flight back to the base at Tibenham, England. Everyone on the ten member crew had to work together to get the plane back to the airfield. Using hand signals and relaying messages between those in the rear and front of the plane, the Williams crew kept busy as they made their way out of enemy territory, all the while keeping their eyes peeled for enemy fighters and flak barrages.

It was noted by Jesse Cummings that by 2:15 PM they were down to 16,000 feet in altitude. The group had dropped 2,000 feet in altitude shortly after the bomb run. By 2:24 PM, the 445th had made it to their Group Rally Point, and at 2:31 PM, they had made it to the Combat Wing Rally Point where

The blue waters of the English Channel and the French coastline just north of Dieppe, France. This is the same view my father's crew saw as they made landfall, and later left enemy airspace along the German occupied French coast. Photo taken by the author as he was on a flight from Edinburgh, Scotland to Paris, France on July 3, 2014. Commercial airlines still fly in the same pattern today.

they reformed as a defensive Combat Wing for maximum fire power from every angle against enemy fighter attacks. There truly was safety in numbers in a Combat Box formation (see Appendix page 140).

At 2:43 PM, they were three miles north of Mannheim, Germany at 15,500 feet, and thankfully, weren't experiencing any flak at that point. They were on course as briefed, but had lost the time gained going into the target. There wasn't much friendly fighter support in evidence, and thankfully there were few enemy fighters showing up. However, they continued to experience accurate and intense flak all through France from small batteries at enemy airdromes and from the cities of Sedan, Abbeville, and Amiens, as they headed for the English Channel.

On plane 447, Sellke noted in his navigator's chart at 3:55 PM (which was probably meant to be noted as 2:55 PM, because he wrote "1555" hours, just before his next entry of "1500" hours), that he saw a B-24 shot down in flames while they were still flying at 15,500 feet. No parachutes were seen, which meant no survivors. The tragic spectacle more than likely shocked him and caused him to be, understandably, off by an hour in his log time entry.

Five friendly fighters joined their formation around 3:15 PM as they were getting near the southwestern border of Belgium and about to cross the French border. The crews breathed sighs of relief as they saw their "little friends" show up. The fighters escorted them the rest of the way across Belgium, through France, and back across the Channel to England. They had flown about five miles north of the town of Sedan in France to avoid flak, passing by it around 3:33 PM. The formation kept a steady speed of 160 mph until about 4:25 PM, when they found themselves just five miles south of Abbeville, France. As they got near that area, they had to speed up to 165 mph and do some weaving to avoid enemy flak as they were flying at 14,000 feet. At 4:30 PM, they crossed the enemy coast just a few miles northeast of Dieppe and two miles south of Le Treport at 14,800 feet altitude without any further enemy opposition. The blue waters of the northern coast of France were a welcome sight and brought a sigh of relief as the English Channel came into view. The Channel was like a blue carpet signaling safety, with England just a few minutes away. Because the lead navigator's radio compass and Gee Box were shot out, Major Stewart turned the lead over to the deputy lead plane on their right, 1st Lt. Conley's plane, *Tenovus*. Conley's crew would guide the formation on instruments back to Tibenham from there. The undercast beneath them covered England, and required precise instrument flying. These were dangerous weather conditions.

The group made it over the Channel in seventeen minutes, and was over Beachy Head, England at 4:47 PM, at an altitude of 10,000 feet. From there the formation proceeded back to the base. The group was over Tibenham at 5:30 PM and had to do a S.O.P. (Standard Operating Procedure) instruments let down through the solid undercast of clouds below them. They were getting sick of the English weather conditions upon returns from missions. Following procedure, they got a radio fix on their designated beacon signal, and circled the signal in formation while over their airfield. One plane at a time peeled-off at 30 second intervals and safely let down through the clouds. When they finally arrived over their home airfield, the Williams crew radio operator Frank Mangan shot a couple of red flares to signal to the ground crews that they had an emergency situation. Mack called the tower and notified them of their dilemma so they would get priority clearance for an emergency landing.

With the hydraulics shot out, it was necessary to hand-crank the main landing gear down, and to give the nose wheel gear a heavy push outward. George was able to get the main gear down and locked. As he did this, the men in the back of the plane had to give him hand signals to let him know that the wheels were down and locked because their communications over the intercom system had been shot out. Yellow tabs appeared near the landing gear which showed when they were locked in place. After crawling into the nose wheel compartment, which only had room enough for one man to crawl into, George then tried to lower the nose wheel by giving it a hard shove. Because he weighed only a 138 pounds and the wheel hundreds of pounds, he was not able to get it fully locked in place. This could spell big trouble during their landing. He informed Mack and Doug about the problem with the nose wheel. It was a pathetical problem with B-24s. George then managed to pinch off a severed hydraulic line with a pair of pliers to give Mack just enough pressure for some brakes. Mack and Doug would also have to use full flaps in the emergency landing.

A SPARKLING, EMERGENCY LANDING

As *Nine Yanks and a Jerk* circled Tibenham Airfield, the pilots used up as much fuel as they could to avoid an explosion. As they were running out of fuel, Mack and Doug prepared to land the damaged plane. George, being the flight engineer, then ordered everyone, except the pilot and co-pilot, to the back of the plane to brace for a risky, tail-dragging landing. The weight of the men in the back of the plane would also help keep the tail section weighed down, as they had to keep as much weight off the nose gear as possible. The tail section was also a safer place to be in during such a situation.

George stood between Mack and Doug and called out the speed and altimeter readings as the two men prepared for the landing. Mack called for Doug to give him full flaps, as they would need to keep the plane's tail end on the ground to keep the weight off the nose wheel. Mack touched the plane down on the edge of the runway at Tibenham at 5:45 PM. *Nine Yanks and a Jerk* rolled down the entire length of the 6,000 foot runway as Mack pulled back on the yoke slightly and Doug kept the flaps down, while the brakes were applied with what was left of the pressure in the brake lines. The tail dragged and sparks flew, while aluminum scars were left all the way down the airstrip. The sound of the metal scraping against the runway was chilling. Muscles tensed. Mack cautiously let the nose of the damaged plane down as they neared the end of the runway. At the right moment, Mack gently applied the brakes as the nose gear touched down. George, still standing between Mack and Doug, warned Mack that the nose wheel wouldn't hold for long once he applied the brakes. Would they wind up smeared all over the runway? The crew wondered if the warbird would hold together, and not allow them to get hurt. Those in the back waited anxiously in their crouched positions. They knew they had to get off of the main runway so that the rest of the group could land safely. They couldn't risk a nose wheel collapse on an active runway with the rest of the group coming in behind them.

As the plane decreased speed, Mack revved up engines three and four and cut back on one and two, and turned to the left to get them onto a narrow taxiway to head toward their hardstand. The men felt a bit calmer. Then, suddenly as they veered left, the nose wheel collapsed. As the wheel collapsed, the tail end abruptly went up into the air like a see-saw, catapulting the men in the back of the plane up to the ceiling and back down, while the plane skidded off the taxiway onto the grassy area beyond it. The battle weary plane and crew came to a grinding stop in the grassy field just off the taxiway.

Nine Yanks and Jerk's nose burrowed into the ground as it skidded to a halt. The sudden stop caused Mack to hit his head on the instrument panel. He received a deep cut on his head from the impact, which left a scar that would still be visible many years later. The shaken crew quickly climbed out of the plane as the emergency vehicles made their way to the site. Amazingly, everyone got out alive

This is a similar view the pilots Mack Williams and Douglas Pillow and flight engineer/top turret gunner George Snook had while *Nine Yanks and a Jerk* made its emergency approach to land on Tibenham's main runway. Photo taken on June 30, 2012 by the author as he was given a flight in the Norfolk Glider Club's tow plane with pilot and club member Tony Griffiths. Our approach was a simulation of the February 25, 1944 landing, without dragging the tail.

On June 25, 2015, Brian Barr and I landed at Tibenham on the same runway. As *Nine Yanks and a Jerk* touched down, even though the runway was over a mile long, they used the length real fast as the tail of the plane was dragged down the entire length of the runway. Sparks flew as they left aluminum scars all the way down it.

Tibenham Airfield from an RAF 1946 Aerial Survey photo. The white arrow shows the emergency landing approach *Nine Yanks and a Jerk* took. Photo courtesy Mike Page.

A composite photograph. The ambulances, men, and background are from a WWII photo from the *NARA*. I inserted a B-24 photo of mine to simulate **Nine Yanks and a Jerk's** approach to Tibenham Airfield on February 25, 1944.

Middle: Two 445th Bomb Group officers, Col. Jones and Lt. Col. Fraser, anxiously watch as planes return from a mission from Tibenham's control tower. These two officers rose to key positions in the 445th BG. Col. Jones eventually took Col. Terrill's place as CO. Photo from Christine (Mangan) Homa via Ron Decker. A formation of B-24s approach as one 'peels off' for a landing. *NARA*. Bottom: This plane is not **Nine Yanks and a Jerk**, but it serves to show the same position a nose wheel collapse left the Williams crew in. *NARA*

HERE IS WHERE *NINE YANKS AND JERK*
SKIDDED OFF OF THE TAXIWAY AFTER
ITS EMERGENCY LANDING WHEN THE
NOSE WHEEL COLLAPSED

without any serious injuries, just a few bumps and a little shaken up. Thanks to the skill of Mack, Doug, George, the rest of the crew, and the grace of God, they all walked away from what could've been a disaster for all. Some of the men kissed the ground and thanked God after they climbed out of the plane. George remarked years later, "Anytime you walk away from a plane safely… that's a good landing!"

Major James "Jimmy" M. Stewart seen here in a photo taken at Tibenham when he was in command of the 703rd Bomb Squadron.

A few minutes earlier, Major Jimmy Stewart and his crew had landed their damaged plane. After he had quickly parked his plane at a nearby hardstand and checked his crew, he immediately got out and ran over to see if the Williams crew was okay. He was the first person to greet them on the airfield. As Stewart approached the rear of the plane that was jutting up into the air, he first met Hank Culver, who was just lighting a cigarette with unsteady hands. Stewart asked him about the safety of the entire crew, in his down-to-earth, reassuring manner. Culver replied, "We're all okay, sir." Stewart then asked him specifically, "Where's Mack?!" Culver responded, "Sir, he's on the other side of the ship," while pointing to the other the other side of the plane with a trembling, freshly lit cigarette in his hand. Stewart looked at him and sympathetically chuckled and then went over to see where Mack was. While in flight, Stewart had seen the .88mm hole on the side of the plane right behind the pilot's seat, and had thought that the pilot, his good buddy Mack Williams, had been killed. Stewart went over to the other

85

side of the ship to see for himself how Williams was, and to take a closer look at the hole in the side of the battle weary plane he had flown in three weeks earlier (see p.107).

Stewart told Williams, in his familiar Pennsylvania accent and tone, "Mack, when I saw that hole in the side of the ship, I thought that you were a goner." After seeing that he and the crew were okay, Stewart congratulated the crew on doing a fine job on getting themselves and the plane back. Mack replied with a response he would later write in his debriefing report – "Thank God for a ten man crew!"

Some other crews came over and walked around the plane and gawked at the size of the hole in the side of the ship, as well as the hundreds of holes that the flak had made. After seeing the damage and hearing the tale from the crew members, they were all amazed that no one was seriously hurt. The crew agreed that they flew with two of the best pilots in the U.S. 8th Air Force – Mack and Doug.

After their debriefing, some of the crew members went back to see the plane with the ground crew. The ground crew chief, Master Sergeant Grant Murray, and his two other ground crew workers each took their turns sticking their heads through the hole and had their pictures taken by George Snook. It became quite a photo op. The most well-known of the photos was that of Grant Murray sticking his head out of the hole (see page 97 for photos).[6] The photo became part of the official news release from the base.

Stewart and Williams went out later that night to celebrate their survival of that mission, and got 'bombed' themselves. They had been scheduled to do a radio interview for the BBC (British Broadcasting Corporation) that evening, but they never made it. Years later, Hank Culver recalled that Stewart and Williams celebrated so much that night that the two of them had to sleep their celebration binge off in hospital beds the next day! The entire day's events and evening celebrations all could've been scenes in one of Jimmy Stewart's dramatic movies (similar in some ways to the dangers and celebrations of flying bombers his post-war film, *Strategic Air Command*), but it was all real.

For many of the crew members the mission was then referred to after that as "Lucky Number 13." It would be a story they would tell to their families, friends, and eager listeners for the rest of their lives. *Nine Yanks and a Jerk* would become a well-known plane among the veterans of the 445th Bomb Group for this mission and for several other reasons as will be explained further in this book. The plane and its crews who flew it would later be known among the various families connected with it, even as of this writing.[7]

---

6. It was a photo I had seen for many years on the internet, but didn't know it was of my father's plane until I began researching and writing this work. It was an incredible discovery.

7. When Mack's daughter, Marlo (Williams) Hillstrom, and I first spoke on the phone, she tested my validity by asking me, "What was *Nine Yanks and a Jerk*?" After I replied correctly, she then knew that I was legitimate in my conversation with her. We get a good laugh out of that story each time we retell our fathers' story to others.

The "Lucky Number 13" ★ For many of the crew the number 13 had some significance. Although many would say that they weren't superstitious, some felt that they might be. The crew left the U.S. on November 13, 1943, flew their first mission on December 13, 1943, and for several men (as mentioned above), this was their 13th mission. Jesse Cummings was born on May 13, 1921, and later graduated from Command and Staff school on a Friday the 13th. When Jesse was a boy one of his cows had two calves born on separate Friday the 13ths. It was a number that he and some of the other crew members were aware of as a reoccurrence in their lives.

Stewart and his men found ways to unwind from the stresses of combat. The pilot of *Nine Yanks and a Jerk*, 1st Lt. William "Mack" Williams (standing at far left) at a sing-along with Major Jimmy Stewart leading the singing and playing the piano in England in 1944 with other combat buddies and some English guests from the Norwich area of England. Photo from a private family collection, courtesy of Marlo (Williams) Hillstrom, daughter of William "Mack" Williams.

NINE YANKS AND A JERK REVISITED YEARS LATER

Many years later after the war, in May of 1988, my father and I went to visit the Pima Air Museum in Tucson, Arizona. We had been out to visit my brother Bill, his wife Janice, and their two daughters Cherise and Michelle in the Phoenix area. Bill suggested that Dad and I make the hour and half drive to visit the museum so that we could see the B-24 Liberator there. Dad was 64 years old at the time, and I was 22. He had not seen a B-24 since the war – over 43 years prior. It would be my first time seeing one in person. We were both excited to go. It was a great suggestion that my brother had made. After touring the inside of the museum, Dad and I walked outside to the desert lot where the Liberator was displayed at the time. When we walked up to it, it was like a moment frozen in time. We both were silent for a few seconds. I felt compelled to break the silence. I asked him the question, "What are you thinking?" I added, "I know that you haven't seen one of these since the war…" He pondered the question for a moment, as he carefully looked over the airframe of the plane. It was like he was seeing an old friend and taking it all in. It also appeared like a flood of memories came across his face. He then affectionately replied, "This is the plane that saved my life. It took a lot of punishment, but brought us home safely from every mission. I wouldn't be standing here today if it weren't for this plane." He went on to describe how their numerous B-24s had been shot up so badly on several missions that they came back with over 300 holes in the ships. He then retold the story of *Nine Yanks and a Jerk* to me. Although he had long forgotten the name of the plane, he told the story of that mission in vivid detail before me and the B-24 we stood in front of. I could see that he was deeply moved by seeing his familiar friend and retelling his combat service in front of it. It had been a long time since he had been this close to one. I felt like I was witnessing the meeting of two war buddies who had not seen each other in a very long time, and who alone understood each other. It was an unforgettable moment that I was honored to be a part of. I know that he was glad to be able to share the experience with me, and I with him. It was a father and son moment that words could not fully express.

My father, Henry J. Culver, Sr. standing in front of the B-24 Liberator at the Pima Air Museum in Tucson, Arizona in May of 1988. Seeing this plane brought back a lot of memories for him. He had not seen one since the end of the war – 43 years before. It was my first time seeing one. It was like witnessing a meeting of two war buddies who had not seen each other in a long time. It was also an opportune teaching moment for him to share his stories with me, from father to son. Author's collection.

MISSION SUMMARY

In a series of files called The Strategic Bombing Survey folders at the National Archives in College Park, Maryland, there is a vast collection of bombing results and an enormous amount of data compiled for every strategic target bombed in Europe by the U.S. Army Air Forces in WWII. The folder for Nuremburg contains the following summary for the results of the February 25, 1944 mission to Nurnberg (referred to as Nuremburg) and nearby Furth.

The narrative is as follows for the Furth target, "This attack caused visible damage to about 30% of the building area, but there was little damage to the larger and more important buildings on the site; the result is likely to be about 2 months' loss of output of aircraft parts and 1-2 months' loss in repairs to aircraft." Six and half weeks later, on April 11, 1944, Allied reconnaissance planes' photos showed that only about "one-quarter of the area of superficial damage had been repaired." The final evaluation also stated,

> "Since the four largest and most important buildings, including machining areas, were relatively undamaged, the target probably retains much of its pre-attack value, but since one-sixth of the building area is structurally damaged, the full pre-attack value is not likely to be regained."

The physical damage to the target had a lot of uncertainty to it since the post-mission reconnaissance photo mission was flown six and a half weeks after the strike. It appeared that about 15% of the building areas were structurally damaged, and another 13% was damaged superficially. The report goes on to say that the "largest buildings, however, which probably housed the most of the vital processes, suffered relatively little damage. The main areas of damage, other than the repair hangar, were the power house, the sheet metal shop, the main stores and two identified workshops."

The main machine shop that was used for component manufacturing was undamaged. A multistory office building received only superficial damage plus 2,000 square feet of structural damage on one edge. Of the two hangars identified with aircraft repairs, the larger was undamaged, although the other was heavily damaged and most of its contents probably ruined.

Six and half weeks after the attack the recon photos showed that the Germans had already cleared some of the structural damage and had repaired some of the superficial damage. Some buildings were getting re-roofed and repaired, while another one had been completely demolished to make way for new construction. It was difficult for Allied analyzers to determine if there was significant loss of future output at this site due to the bombing raid because they didn't have enough information available regarding "the kinds and quantities of aircraft parts produced at this factory." The best they could determine was that about two months loss of aircraft parts and one to two months of aircraft repairs was "likely to have been caused." The report concluded that the loss of output of completed Me 110s at the Bachmann factory "is not likely to be increased substantially by this attack. However, fewer components will be available for repair, and assembly of aircraft in the future, as a result of this damage."

It was also hard to determine aircraft losses on the ground due to the raid because a month and a half had elapsed between the raid and the reconnaissance photos that were taken. It would not be the last raid of the war on this target, however. The Eighth Air Force would have to strike it a second time as some of the buildings were rebuilt and had become operational again.

A strike photo taken by a 392nd Bomb Group B-24 on February 25, 1944 over the German airfield at Furth. This is the view the Williams crew and all crews flying to this target would've basically seen. The center of the airfield was the aiming point for the 445th Bomb Group. The 392nd Bomb Group was part of the same bomber stream with the Second Air Division. Photo from http://www.b24.net/ books/furth.htm and *NARA*.

The Me110 factory at Furth, which was rebuilt, needed to be bombed again a year later after the February 25, 1944 mission. The above 1945 photo shows the damage to the hangar that was blown sky high on the later raid. Only dents were given to the noses of the Me110s in the foreground. *NARA*

AN IRONY IN AN INFAMOUS REGION

In November of 1945, about a year and nine months after the raid, and about six months after the war in Europe ended, the Nuremberg Trials were held about four miles to the southeast of the factory and airfield that was bombed at Furth. The Allied-held trials put surviving political and military Nazi war criminals on the stand at the Palace of Justice (ironically-named) in the city of Nuremburg. The Soviets had wanted to put the Nazis on trial in Berlin because it was the capital of Nazi Germany. However, the western Allies, especially the Americans, chose the Nuremberg site because the building was spacious and had a large prison as part of the complex, and it was also in the American zone of occupation. The complex was still largely intact, having survived the extensive Allied bombings of the region. In addition, there was some stark, ironic symbolism involved. Nuremburg was considered to be the ceremonial birthplace of the Nazi (National Socialist) Party, also known as "The Party" among the Germans.

In 1933, Hitler held the "Rally of Victory" at the Nazi Party's rally grounds in the city of Nuremburg to celebrate the party's "Victory" over the Weimar Republic. The annual Nazi rallies from 1933-1938 became known in English as the Nuremberg Rallies. The Nazis had chosen Nuremberg because of its central location within the German Reich, and so made use of the large parkway named "Luitpoldhain" (literally translated: "Luitpold grove", named after Luitpold, Prince Regent of Bavaria) which had existed there since 1906. Hitler had a huge grandstand built there that was about 500 feet long, could sit 500 dignitaries, and had two twenty foot high gold eagles at each end. The edifice became the first permanent Nazi structure built in Nuremberg.

During the Nuremberg Trials, Hermann Goring, the German Commander of the Luftwaffe, was convicted and sentenced to death by hanging as determined by the Allied court at the Palace of Justice. Earlier, Goring had been the second highest-ranking member of the Nazi Party and was chosen by Hitler to be his successor. Goring, however, had fallen out of favor with Hitler when his Luftwaffe couldn't prevent Allied bombs from falling on Berlin. Humiliated by his upcoming death sentence, Goring chose rather to commit suicide by taking a cyanide pill that was smuggled into his cell the night before he was to be executed, rather than be hanged publicly. The Palace of Justice in Nuremberg thus became the fitting place for the final demise of the Nazis, and their notorious Luftwaffe commander.

The author in front of a captured German .88mm anti-aircraft flak gun at the National WWII Museum in New Orleans, Louisiana. German cities and industrial areas were fortified with dozens of these heavy pieces of artillery. Nurnberg had quite a few as part of its defenses. It was a gun like this which fired the shell that blew through my father's plane on February 25, 1944. Photo taken on April 15, 2014.

HITLER'S REICH IN RUINS

Left: Hitler and a Nazi Party rally at Nuremberg, August 1933. Right: The Nuremberg Trials looking down on the defendants' dock, c.1945-46. Hermann Goring is seated in the foreground directly in front of the MP whose back is to the camera. Goring, the former Commander of the Luftwaffe, committed suicide the night before he was to be executed for his crimes against humanity as the second highest-ranking Nazi under Hitler. Below: Sections of Nuremberg after the many Allied bombings at the war's end. The devastation was typical of most German cities that were pounded by such attacks throughout the war. Hitler's Reich was ruined. *NARA*

703rd Bomb Squadron Patch, 445th Bomb Group

Quotes from Jimmy Stewart and the Williams Crew about the Mission

"Flak: Moderate and accurate along course from enemy coast to Rhine River. Moderate and accurate over target – they tracked us around our turn after bombs away. Small batteries located near airports which we passed over on way out were pretty good shots."
Major James M. Stewart, Group Leader, 445th Bomb Group, 703rd Squadron commander, from the Group Leader's Report of Mission 25 February 1944.

"I'm up in the top turret, and he [Frank] is on my immediate right, at his [radio] desk, and that shell coming up underneath me, and pretty damn close to him, and hitting the armor plating behind the pilot... was close.

When that shell hit that armor [plating] behind the pilot, it took that great big hunk of steel and pushed it right down in the bomb bay. I don't remember whether it took the bomb bay out, or whether we opened the bomb bay and dropped it. The bombs were gone. There were no bombs aboard. It also took my packed parachute and boots right out the hole!

I always say, thank God it was made by slave labor and it didn't go off. Fortunately it was built by slave labor and it was a dud. Had it been live, we wouldn't have been talking – we would've been blown sky high in a minute, which I've seen happen numerous times over my period of time serving overseas.

As soon as we got down to lower altitudes where I could see the problem then I knew how severe it was. That's when the pilot and I got into a discussion on about how severe it was. Now, I did attempt to pitch off the [hydraulic] lines so that he could have brakes and flaps one time, and the fluid would leak through the pitch lines I had made. And then we were done. Once we were on the ground I didn't care. The main line to the main wheels was gone completely. We couldn't do anything about that. We had what we called

Jimmy Stewart wrote the Group Leader's report for the February 25, 1944 mission to bomb Nurnberg/Furth, Germany.

"Accumulating Pressure" in the front, so it would build up in a round ball. So, we did have some pressure that we could use for brakes and flaps, but we couldn't use anything on the main strut.

All I can say is, I took one look and said, "We got a lot of problems."

When it [the shell] hit, it also took out an electrical box that fed to the rear of the aircraft. We not only lost hydraulics, we lost some of our communications system at the same time, so most of the stuff was done verbally [i.e. face to face] from there on. We couldn't talk to the people in the rear [of the plane] at all. That's the reason when they gave us the "Thumbs up" - it was a visual sign that the wheels were down and locked, because we couldn't communicate with each other.

The main thing is that it took out some of our hydraulic system, which was the biggest factor that we had. There again, with a little engineering, we brought her back. Well, we got the main gear down... that was no problem, 'cause that's just a manual function. But the biggest problem was the damn nose wheel – it was just too heavy to get out and locked.

When the main strut was cranked down, two yellow bits would lock in place, and the crew in the back could see that (and of course we were in the catwalk and we didn't have oxygen on because we were below 10,000 feet), so, at that point in time, they could give me the signal: "down and locked." Then, we did try to get the nose wheel out and were not successful. I then ordered everyone, except the pilot and co-pilot, to the back of the plane. This would put most of the weight in the back of the plane so that we could drag the tail and keep the weight off of the nose. That's when we landed and the nose wheel collapsed. We touched down on a normal landing with our main wheels, and the pilot pulled back on the stick slightly, and we dragged it. He dragged it down the runway until we lost speed, and then he turned off on a small runway that would take us to where we were parking the plane. And when he turned off, that's when the nose wheel collapsed. Soon as he put some weight forward, it collapsed right away. Jimmy Stewart came up to see how we were. He was the first one to meet us when we crawled out.

I had to give my pilot, William "Mack" a hell of a lot of credit. He'd done everything right. He brought that damn airplane in tail-heavy, dragged her right down the runway ('cause I already told him soon as he put on the nose it was gonna collapse, and my prediction was right). We turned off the main runway and the damn thing collapsed... which I knew would happen, and he knew it too. He took my word for what was gonna happen.

Everyone had done their share. There wasn't any discussion or argument with anybody. I was in charge of that damn airplane, and no one ever argued with me one bit, even Mack, he never argued with me. If I told him something, he said, "Okay."

Williams... had done a superb job of following my little instructions to the tee, and it worked. He and I had worked together on that bit... and it worked!

We accomplished what we had to do, and we landed and walked away... and that's a good landing!"
Tech Sergeant George Snook, Flight Engineer/Top Turret Gunner, from phone conversations in 2011 and 2012, at ages 90 and 91.

"One terrible mission way in Germany to Nurnberg. No fighters. [An] .88mm shell missed me. Tore floor up and side of ship. Blew my chute out. Only the Lord saved us that day."
Tech Sergeant Frank Mangan, Radio Operator, from his diary entry on February 25, 1944

"We took our longest one into Germany yet and just after bombs away a flak shell came through the

bottom of the plane, through the floor of the flight deck about two feet from my feet and it went into an instrument box and tore the side of the plane out.

The Colonel (Colonel Robert H. Terrill) and the Major (Major James M. "Jimmy" Stewart of film and air force fame) asked if I got hurt. The major dresses next to me in the locker room. When we came in, he just looked at me and said: "When I see you I wonder how in the Lord's name you are still alive."

[The] shell... tore the handle off my chute and blew the chute right through the side of the plane. I still have the handle. The chute is in Germany some place.

We made an emergency landing as our hydraulic system was shot out."
Tech Sergeant Frank Mangan, Radio Operator, from the *Binghamton Sun* newspaper article quoting a personal letter written to his parents, 1944.

"When we were starting on our 13th mission over Germany, some of us thought it might be a good idea to refer to it simply as 12-B, but the pilot pooh-poohed the idea. That day, though, we ran into more trouble than on any of the other previous ones.

The ship was hit by an .88mm shell, which fortunately failed to explode. If it had, I probably wouldn't be here telling this. After that experience, our pilot admitted that perhaps he should have called it 12-B. It might have been safer. But that was an extreme case. I'm not usually very superstitious."
Tech Sergeant Frank Mangan, Radio Operator, from the *Binghamton Sun* newspaper interview, June 27, 1945.

"We got hit by what the Germans called an 88 millimeter. It came right up on the inside of my foot and went out the side of the plane." **Tech Sergeant Frank Mangan, Radio Operator, from *The Tampa Tribune* newspaper interview, January 26, 1989.**

"We got hit by anti-aircraft fire... it took out our hydraulic system. And behind the pilot there's a half-inch armor plating that protects him. It [the .88mm shell] took the armor plating off, from behind the pilot. It didn't explode. It just went through the ship, and the debris from the flight deck went back (and I was at the waist gun that day firing at an enemy) and it took the post sight right off of my gun and took the machine gun right out of my hands.

I never thought, well, how can I put this?... I was not afraid at any time because I was so busy trying to do things mechanically, I didn't have time to think that I was scared. But, luckily, I figured, well, the Lord must've had other plans for me, because I'm here today.

We had so many holes in the ship, and the hydraulics system was shot out. So, the first engineer... [went] down by the nose [to] crank the nose wheel down. Automatically, it's done by the hydraulics system, but being that we had no hydraulics system, [he] had to do it by hand. And you only have a little space like this [about a foot and a half, he showed with his hands] to get up there and crank this big nose wheel down. Well, the first engineer ... went down and ... did some cranking down, but by that time we found a spot in the clouds [to go through as] we were going to land. I expected the worst. So we were on the runway... and we turned [veering left onto a small taxiway, and then] the nose wheel collapsed. In the meantime, he had cut some of the engine speed back, and we were fortunate enough that those in the back hit the ceiling of the plane, the roof of the plane, and come landing down, but we all got out okay.

Jimmy Stewart was our wingman that day, and he landed right behind us. I got out and lit a cigarette, and was shaking like this [trembling hands] with the cigarette, and he came around the plane and he said, "Where's Mack? (Which was my pilot, and they were good buddies.) And I said, "Sir, he's on the other side of the ship." And I'm going like this [pointing to the other side with a shaking finger]. He looked at me and he laughed. He goes around, and he sees my pilot and says, "Mack, when I saw that hole in the side of the ship, I thought that you were a goner."

We had a big gaping hole. It looked like a third window on the ship. So, we all came out okay. So, it just happened that night that he and my pilot... went out on 'a bender'. I won't forget that because they were supposed to go and broadcast for the BBC, and they never made it. They got so 'bombed' that they had to get a bed in the hospital to sleep it off until the next day.
Staff Sergeant Hank Culver, Sr., Left Waist Gunner, from a video interview with his son Scott on June 13, 2000.

"What damage the enemy fighters failed to do, the usual amount of flak along the route caused some concern. Flying alongside another aircraft, a ground shell neatly clipped off a propeller. It continued to fly on three propellers. About the same time another shell came up through our aircraft in the area [right behind] the pilot.

The shell didn't explode but went clear through the flight deck taking an extra parachute with it. No one was hurt, but slightly scared. The bombs had already gone to the ground. Everyone looked around. The engines continued to purr as if nothing happened. The intercom system had been knocked out so nobody could communicate with each other.

When it was possible, a check was made of the damage. The shell had severed the main hydraulic line under the flight deck, splintered a radio set, tore the thick armor plating from its moorings [from behind the pilot's seat], and damaged another parachute.

The trip back to Tibenham was uneventful. No one said much, partly because what had happened earlier. The danger was not over. With no hydraulic fluid, there was the danger of crashing when an attempt was made to land. Most of the gas had been used up, so the damaged aircraft flew around the base until the balance of fuel had been almost used up.

The base fire department was alerted and came to our rescue. Snook lowered the landing gear by hand and Williams successfully landed but the tail end of the plane raised up in the air when the wheel section collapsed.

Everyone jumped out and literally kissed the ground, and thanked the Lord they were safe. The maintenance people took over and began repairs so it could be used again."
Staff Sergeant Joe Minton, Tail Gunner, from his book, *Ten Men and a Bomber*, p.34.

"It was a good thing that shell was a dud or somebody might have been hurt." **Staff Sergeant Billy Fields, Right waist gunner, from Coal Grove, Ohio newspaper article in 1944.**

"On our 13th mission we got shot up pretty bad, but luckily we made it home." **Lt. Jesse Cummings, from an audio interview with his daughter Penny in 1994.**

"Thank God for a 10-man crew!" **Lt. William M. "Mack" Williams, from 25 February 1944 Debriefing Report.**

A Few Words about the Ground Crew Chief – Grant Murray

"He was an excellent crew chief. When we brought the ship back we'd have a short discussion of the things we felt needed checked, and whatever it was, Sergeant Murray handled it expertly. Never had a problem with anything we talked about. It was done, and done correctly. Now he had help. This [ground crew] wasn't a single person. He had two or three other mechanics who could help him with a problem. He was a good person."

Tech Sergeant George Snook, Flight Engineer/Top Turret Gunner, from phone a conversation on January 3, 2012, at age 91.

That's a Good Landing!

The ground crew chief, M/Sgt. Grant Murray (left photo) is shown sticking his head through the hole the .88mm shell had made. [It was Murray, not Petterson (see photo on next page).] The photo was taken shortly after the plane made the emergency landing at their base in Tibenham, England on February 25, 1944. Murray and the rest of the ground crew (shown in the other two photos sticking their heads through the same hole) had their work cut out for themselves as they had to repair the battle-damaged plane and restore it to flight worthy condition. The plane was repaired and did go on to fly other combat missions, but not with the Williams crew. Other crews flew it from then on. It was eventually shot down by German fighters with another crew flying it (see page 109 below) on the mission of April 12, 1944. The Williams crew was flying to its right as they watched the plane go down in flames. It crashed in a field in Belgium. Eight of the crew members survived the attack. There is a memorial marker at the crash site today. Photo at left courtesy of George Snook. Photos at right courtesy of Jane (Fields) Deeds via Dan Deeds.

NEWS RELEASES ABOUT THE MISSION

The official 1944 press releases from the 445th Bomb Group at Tibenham Airfield, England for the February 25, 1944 mission to Nurnberg, Germany, which was also included in local newspapers back in the States. From the *445th Bomb Group folders, National Archives*. (See following pages also.)

STORY NUMBER 50

AN EIGHTH AAF LIBERATOR STATION,ENGLAND

THE CREW OF THE LIBERATOR "NINE YANKS AND A JERK" WHO ARE MEMBERS OF COL. ROBERT H. TERRILLIS LIBERATOR GROUP, HAD QUITE A THRILL ON THE FURTH MISSION TO GERMANY A FEW DAYS AGO. T/SGT. FRANK MANGAN OF BRINGHAMTON, NEW YORK, RADIO OPERATOR, WAS RIGHT IN THE MIDDLE OF THE WHOLE AFFAIR.

SHORTLY AFTER THE GROUP HAD BOMBED THE TARGET THE FORMATION WAS TURNING TO AVOID A FLAK AREA. IT WAS ABOUT HALF WAY THRU THE TURN WHEN AN 88MM SHELL CAME FLYING THRU THE "NINE YANKS" WITH A "JERK". THE FLOOR OF THE B-24 WAS RIPPED APART, THE RADIO SET WAS CUT IN TOO. THE ARMOR PLATING FROM THE BACK OF THE PILOTS SEAT WAS KNOCKED OFF AND CAME OUT THE SIDE OF THE SHIP. THE GROUND CREW CHIEF M/SGT. EUGENE L. PETTERSON OF 518 W. MAIN ST., OSHKOSH, WIS. IS SEEN POKING HIS HEAD OUT OF THE HOLE MADE BY THE SHELL.

PARTS OF THE TORN PLANE CAUGHT IN THE SLIP STREAM AND HIT THE LEFT WAIST GUN AND KNOCKED OFF THE FRONT SIGHT. THE RADIO OPERATORS PARACHUTE WAS BLOWN OPEN AND OUT THE HOLE WHILE ANOTHER PARACHUTE WAS HIT SO HARD THAT IT POPPED OPEN ON THE FLIGHT DECK WHICH ADDED TO THE CONFUSSION. CONSIDERABLE OTHER DAMAGE WAS DONE INCLUDING KNOCKING OUT THE HYDRAULIC SYSTEM.

IT WAS THE 13TH MISSION FOR THREE OF THE MEN. THE RIGHT WAIST GUNNER, BILLIE G. FIELDS OF IRONTON, OHIO, NAVIGATOR 2ND LT JESSE M. CUMMINGS OF LAKE CHARLES, LA. AND THE ABOVE MENTIONED RADIO OPERATOR. ACCORDING TO SGT MANGAN "IT WAS A GOOD THING THAT SHELL WAS A DUD OR SOMEBODY MIGHT HAVE BEEN HURT" OTHER MEMBERS OF THE CREW WERE GLAD IT WAS A DUD, BUT CONSIDERED THE DAMAGE BAD ENOUGH TO SUIT THEM.

——— END ———

Coal Grove Waist Gunner Had Thrill On Bombing Run

AN EIGHTH AAF LIBERATOR STATION, England— The crew of the Liberator "Nine Yanks and a Jerk" who are members of Col. Robert H. Terrillis Liberator group, had quite a thrill on a mission to Germany a few days ago.

Shortly after the group had bombed the target the formation was turning to avoid a flak area. It was about half way through the turn when an 88 mm. shell came flying through the "Nine Yanks" with a "Jerk." The floor of the B-24 was ripped apart, the radio set was cut in too. The armor plating from the back of the pilots seat was knocked off and came out the side of the ship.

Parts of the torn plane caught in the slip stream and hit the left waist gun and knocked off the front sight. The radio operators parachute was blown open and out the hole while another parachute was hit so hard that it popped open on the flight deck adding to the confusion. Other damage done included knocking out the hydraulic system.

It was the 13th mission for three of the men: The right waist gunner, Billie G. Fields of Coal Grove; Navigator 2nd Lieut. Jesse M. Cummings of Lake Charles, La., and the above mentioned radio operator. According to Sgt. Fields, "It was a good thing that shell was a dud or somebody might have been hurt." Other members of the crew were glad it was a dud, but considered the damage bad enough to suit them.

Above: Billy Fields at Tibenham Airfield. Below; Coal Grove, Ohio newspaper from Billy Fields' personal collection. Courtesy Jane (Fields) Deeds and Dan Deeds.

Sergt. Mangan's Plane Ripped Badly on His 13th Mission

Tech. Sergt. Frank A. Mangan, Jr., 22, of Binghamton, and the crew of the Liberator, "Nine Yanks and a Jerk," had quite a thrill on a mission to Germany a few days ago, according to a delayed release from an Eighth A. A. F. Liberator Station in England.

Hit by flak, the craft was badly battered, so much so that the pilot was compelled to make an emergency landing.

By coincidence, Sergeant Mangan, a radio operator, outlined some of the details of the perilous flight in a letter to his parents, Mr. and Mrs. Frank A. Mangan, Sr., 56 Murray Street.

Explaining that it was his thirteenth mission, he wrote in part:

"Billy (Navigator William G. Fields, Ironton, Ohio) and I are over the half way now.

"We took our longest one into Germany yet and just after bombs away a flak shell came through the bottom of the plane, through the floor of the flight deck about two feet from my feet and it went into an intrument box and tore the side of the plane out.

"The colonel (Col. Robert H. Terrillis) and the major (Maj. James M. 'Jimmy' Stewart of film and air force fame) asked if I got hurt.

"The major dresses next to me in the locker room.

"When we came in, he just looked at me and said: 'When I see you I wonder how in the Lord's name you are still alive.'

"A shell which blew up inside the plane tore the handle off my chute and blew the chute right through the side of the plane. I still have the handle. The chute is in Germany some place.

"We made an emergency landing as our hydraulic system was shot out."

Sergeant Mangan served in the same training unit with Major Stewart. Later they both went overseas in the same unit.

Additional details of the flight are given in the A. A. F. release which reads in part:

"Shortly after the group had bombed the target the formation was turning to avoid a flak area. It was about half way through the turn when an 88mm shell came flying through the 'Nine Yanks and a Jerk.' The floor of the B-24 was ripped apart, the radio set was cut in two. The armor plating from the back of the pilot's seat was knocked off and came out the side of the ship.

"Parts of the torn plane caught in the slip stream and hit the left waist gun and knocked off the front sight. The radio operator's parachute was blown open and out the hole while another parachute was hit so hard that it popped open on the flight deck, adding to the confusion. Other damage included the knocking out of the hydraulic system."

Sergeant Mangan and his brother, First Class Private Robert A. Mangan, recently met in England, according to a cablegram just received by their parents. Robert has been overseas since last month and is serving with an anti-aircraft unit.

In another letter, the sergeant, who has been decorated with the Air Medal and two Oak Leaf Clusters for meritorious achievements in bombing missions, wrote that he had a "good look at the King and Queen" and that Princess Elizabeth is "not bad at all."

Above: *Binghamton Sun* newspaper, Binghamton, New York. From Frank Mangan's collection.
Courtesy Christine (Mangan) Homa via Ron Decker.

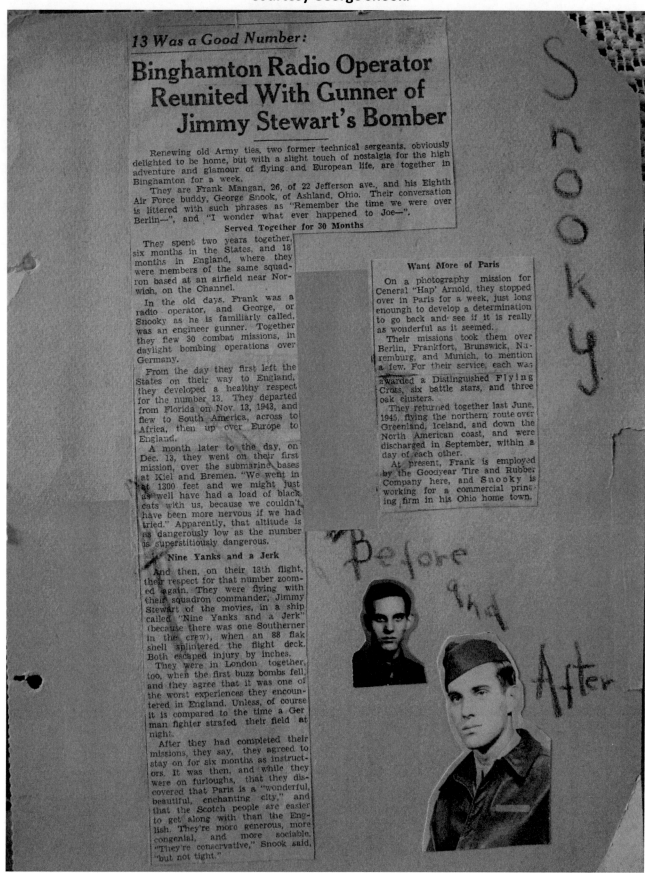

13 Was a Good Number:

Binghamton Radio Operator Reunited With Gunner of Jimmy Stewart's Bomber

Renewing old Army ties, two former technical sergeants, obviously delighted to be home, but with a slight touch of nostalgia for the high adventure and glamour of flying and European life, are together in Binghamton for a week.

They are Frank Mangan, 26, of 22 Jefferson ave., and his Eighth Air Force buddy, George Snook, of Ashland, Ohio. Their conversation is littered with such phrases as "Remember the time we were over Berlin—", and "I wonder what ever happened to Joe—".

Served Together for 30 Months

They spent two years together, six months in the States, and 18 months in England, where they were members of the same squadron based at an airfield near Norwich, on the Channel.

In the old days, Frank was a radio operator, and George, or Snooky as he is familiarly called, was an engineer gunner. Together they flew 30 combat missions, in daylight bombing operations over Germany.

From the day they first left the States on their way to England, they developed a healthy respect for the number 13. They departed from Florida on Nov. 13, 1943, and flew to South America, across to Africa, then up over Europe to England.

A month later to the day, on Dec. 13, they went on their first mission, over the submarine bases at Kiel and Bremen. "We went in at 1300 feet and we might just as well have had a load of black cats with us, because we couldn't have been more nervous if we had tried." Apparently, that altitude is as dangerously low as the number is superstitiously dangerous.

Nine Yanks and a Jerk

And then, on their 13th flight, their respect for that number zoomed again. They were flying with their squadron commander, Jimmy Stewart of the movies, in a ship called "Nine Yanks and a Jerk" (because there was one Southerner in the crew), when an 88 flak shell splintered the flight deck. Both escaped injury by inches.

They were in London together, too, when the first buzz bombs fell, and they agree that it was one of the worst experiences they encountered in England. Unless, of course it is compared to the time a German fighter strafed their field at night.

After they had completed their missions, they say, they agreed to stay on for six months as instructors. It was then, and while they were on furloughs, that they discovered that Paris is a "wonderful, beautiful, enchanting city," and that the Scotch people are easier to get along with than the English. They're more generous, more congenial, and more sociable. "They're conservative," Snook said, "but not tight."

Want More of Paris

On a photography mission for Ceneral "Hap" Arnold, they stopped over in Paris for a week, just long enough to develop a determination to go back and see if it is really as wonderful as it seemed.

Their missions took them over Berlin, Frankfort, Brunswick, Nuremburg, and Munich, to mention a few. For their service, each was awarded a Distinguished Flying Cross, six battle stars, and three oak clusters.

They returned together last June, 1945, flying the northern route over Greenland, Iceland, and down the North American coast, and were discharged in September, within a day of each other.

At present, Frank is employed by the Goodyear Tire and Rubber Company here, and Snooky is working for a commercial printing firm in his Ohio home town.

THE EFFECTS OF BIG WEEK: BIG "B" – BERLIN – AND BEYOND

"Hitler built a fortress around Europe, but he forgot to put a roof on it." - President Franklin D. Roosevelt

The results of the Big Week raids were a turning point in the air war over Europe, especially over Germany. Although the USAAF was initially concerned about the losses of heavy bombers during the campaign (fearing the loss of possibly 200 per day), they lost 137 during the entire week. The introduction of the long-range escort fighters changed the tide of the air war for both the bombers and their crews, as well as what the German Air Force would experience. Doolittle's command to allow the American fighter pilots to pursue the German fighter pilots achieved significant results. As a result of that week's exploits, the German Luftwaffe lost over 355 fighter planes and about 150 of its pilots, many of whom were seasoned veterans. This was a big blow to the German Air Force. The week resulted in a step forward in the Allied gain of air superiority over Europe. Adolf Galland, the inspector general of the Luftwaffe's fighters, was compelled to say that they had lost some of their best squadron and group commanders. He was quoted as saying, "Each incursion of the enemy is costing us some fifty aircrewmen. The time has come when our weapon (the Luftwaffe) is in sight of collapse" (*Big Week*: *Six Days That Changed the Course of WWII*, Yenne, p.230).

The losses of American crews in early 1944, although still high, was lower than its 1943 rates. With the constant arrival and steady stream of new bomber crews and bombers, and fighter pilots and fighter planes, the strategic and tactical forces of the U.S. Army Air Forces continued to grow. Instead of being on the defensive all the time and trying to avoid the German Luftwaffe, now the USAAF would be on the offensive and attempt to draw the German fighter pilots up to engage its fighter pilots with the Allied ones, with the intent to destroy the enemy's air force by attrition.

The Big Week raids also created a crisis for the German aircraft industry. Although the loss of German aircraft production was not crippling, it was significant and extensive. During Big Week, the 8th Air Force so damaged the Messerschmitt plant at Regensburg that it was rendered permanently inoperable. The plant at Augsburg stopped aircraft production for two weeks. The Leipzig plant had "160 new aircraft damaged, while at Gotha 74 aircraft were damaged or destroyed." Some estimates are that the Germans lost the production of over 750 fighters. Another result of the Big Week raids was that the German aircraft production industry dispersed its production plants from "27 main airplane plants to 729 small plants… and 59 aircraft-engine plants would be dispersed to 249 locations even though this industry had not yet been attacked on the scale of the assembly plants" (*Operation Pointblank: Defeating the Luftwaffe*, Zaloga, p.71-72). By dispersing production in such ways, the assembling of aircraft fell prey to lower quality of supervision, needs for a greater work force (which was already strained), transportation difficulties for parts and assembly components, and more opportunity for sabotage by slave or forced labor. The effects would be a lower quality of aircraft production.

Additional results were that the 8th Air Force planners would now be able to plan operations and attacks deeper into Germany, even to the most heavily defended targets. In a matter of two weeks, masses of American heavy bombers, along with their fighter escorts would reach Big "B" – Berlin. On March 3, 1944, the 8th Air Force launched its first attack against Berlin. Although weather forced most of the attack force to return, 31 Flying Fortresses made it over the target. Two days later, on March 6th, over 800 heavy bombers and 800 fighters reached the German capital. The Williams crew was on both raids. My father said to me (over 50 years later) about the March 6th mission: "The Germans threw everything up at us, except the kitchen sink. I looked out my waist gun window and saw over 1,000 planes in the sky. It was an amazing sight. To know that I was part of it was an incredible experience. I'll never forget it."

Above: B-24s in a flak barrage. The Germans threw everything up at them over Berlin. (L) The US military newspaper *Stars and Stripes* announces the first US daylight bombing raid on Berlin in March of 1944. (R) The P-51 Mustang with long-range drop tanks – the 'game-changer' in the air war over Europe. *NARA*

By D-Day, June 6, 1944, the Germans had withdrawn their fighter units back toward Germany. As a result of these heavy losses, along with Hitler's poor decisions at the time, they could only put up two fighters within sight of the invasion forces. General Dwight Eisenhower, who was in command of Operation Overlord, said this of American and Allied air power in relation to the Allied landings in his D-Day message, *"But this is the year 1944! Much has happened since the Nazi triumphs of 1940-41. The United Nations have inflicted upon the Germans great defeats, in open battle, man-to-man. Our air offensive has seriously reduced their strength in the air and their capacity to wage war on the ground."* He understood well what air power had accomplished and what would mean to our ground troops in the landings.

General Eisenhower

Nine Yanks and a Jerk's Original Crew

Lt. Earle Metcalf's crew

Back Row, left to right:
T/Sgt. James R. Crawford - Engineer
2nd Lt. Paul G. W. Fischer - Navigator
2nd Lt. John E. Lercari - Co-Pilot
2nd Lt. Earle G. Metcalf - Pilot
2nd Lt. Ernest H. Hutton - Bombardier

Front Row, left to right:
S/Sgt. Don C. Dewey - Engineer Gunner
S/Sgt. Stanley W. Treusch - Armorer/Gunner
S/Sgt. William K. Timmons - Armorer/Gunner
S/Sgt. Phillip Bronstein - Radio Operator
S/Sgt. Earl T. Doggett - Engineer Gunner
Sgt. Eugene Peterson – Ground Crew Chief

This original 703rd Squadron crew went down in the North Sea in another plane, #42-7523 ***Billie Babe***,* at the start of the mission to Syracourt, France on February 2, 1944. Metcalf's crew was in the same element of the formation with the Williams crew on that fateful day. No one knew for sure what happened to cause the plane to go down. Was it a mechanical problem? Metcalf's plane was last seen going down through a cloud bank over England on the way to an assembly point before leaving the English coast. They disappeared without a trace. The crew was presumed to have gone down in the North Sea. One of the gunners on the plane, Earl Doggett, had a premonition of his death the day before the mission, which he had shared with his fellow 703rd Squadron buddy Harold "Robbie" Robinson. Robinson tried to convince him otherwise, but Doggett was insistent that he knew it was his time. Robinson wrote in his book, *A Reason to Live* (1988), "Could it be possible that he had a real premonition of what was coming?" p.267. The crew's disappearance was a tragic example of the realities of war and the sudden loss of friends who shared Nissen hut quarters.

---

* The Williams crew had also flown in this plane on two previous missions.   Photo courtesy of Charlie Doggett.

Many crews who shared a hut with another crew often saw empty cots opposite theirs after some missions. Replacement crews would soon arrive and the process would repeat itself. It was rare that a crew completed its 30 combat missions. As mentioned previously, my father's crew, the William's crew, was one of only six original crews to complete their 30 missions from the original 16 crews that were with the 703rd Squadron. They lost 63% of their original squadron's crews and planes - 100 men were missing.

How *Nine Yanks and a Jerk* Got Its Name

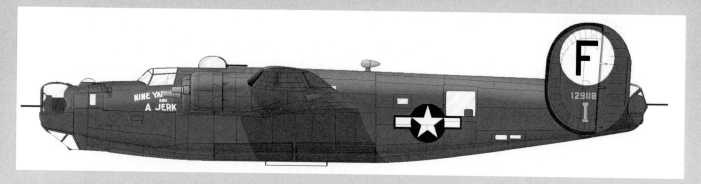

B-24H Liberator   Serial Number 41-29118   Manufactured at Consolidated/Fort Worth

While perusing internet search results for the name of the B-24 Liberator *Nine Yanks and a Jerk* in April of 2012, I stumbled across an article quoted below. Of all places, I saw that it was from my own 'backyard' in New Jersey. An article from a Rutgers University interview with a former 445th Bomb Group, 703rd Bomb Squadron member, Mr. Walter Scott Buist held on September 27, 1995 at Rutgers University, in New Brunswick, New Jersey revealed the reason for the plane's somewhat enigmatic

T/Sgt. Walter Scott Buist in front of *Nine Yanks and a Jerk* sometime before its fateful mission on April 12, 1944. Buist served at Tibenham as a ground crew chief, a specialist who also worked with the top secret Norden bomb sight, and also as a spare flight engineer and top turret gunner when needed. Courtesy the Buist family.

namesake. Mr. Buist served at the same base in Tibenham, England as my father and his crew did, and the original crew of *Nine Yanks and a Jerk*. Mr. Buist was a flight engineer who was not assigned to a permanent crew, but who worked with the ground crews on the B-24 Liberator bombers. He was also on flying status as a flight engineer and a qualified gunner and could fly with a crew as a replacement if they needed someone to fill in for a gunner and/or a flight engineer who couldn't make a mission for whatever reasons. He also was a specialist in calibrating the famed Norden Bomb Sight for the lead planes.

Below is his quote from an audio taped interview session. After he was asked about being on the famous low-level, dangerous mission to the Ploesti oil fields in Romania in the summer of 1943 (flown from an army air base in North Africa),* Mr. Buist explained how he was then later assigned to the 445th Bomb Group as part of the 703rd Bomb Squadron, under Jimmy Stewart's command in the latter part of that same year:

> Yes. … Then, we immediately went up to East Anglia and were assigned to the Eighth Air Force, 445th Bomb Group, 703rd Bomb Squadron. … That first mission there was with James Stewart. In fact, … my sister, Jenny, … was in high school at this point, and she used to say, in her letters to me, "Get me some more of Jimmy Stewart's autographs. All the girls want them. All the girls want Jimmy Stewart's autograph." [laughter] So, of course, every time you got a pass or any document like that, he was signing it, as my squadron commander. I was sending home five or six Jimmy Stewart autographs with every other letter. Pages 21-22

> There's one crew that I flew with on two missions, where we had one guy on board from Biloxi, on this ship, and I had nothing to do with naming the plane, but, the plane was named, *Nine Yanks and a Jerk*. [laughter] The rest were all New England boys and this one guy, who was a sugar cane guy, from somewhere down in the bayou someplace. … I flew flight engineer. Their flight engineer got hit badly. … In fact, he lost one eye and had his head tore up a bit. Until they got a replacement in, I flew twice with them, [in the] Martin upper [turret, as the] flight engineer on that ship. I had a picture taken with [them] that got in the paper one time, [laughter] because we did good, …. Page 19 from http://oralhistory.rutgers.edu/images/PDFs/buist_w_scott.pdf

It appears that the mystery has been finally solved. Here is an eyewitness who flew with the original crew. He is correct on a few points, but slightly off on others (most likely due to the many years between the interview and the events). The Missing Aircrew Report #2509 (now at the National Archives), which was filled out for this crew when they went missing on the February 2, 1944 mission to Syracourt, France, shows most of the original crew members' home addresses. It verifies that most were northerners on the crew, but not all were New Englanders, and the one original southerner was from Arkansas. At any rate, the presumption seems quite well confirmed that this is how the plane was named.

*Prior to being assigned to the 445th BG, T/Sgt. Buist flew on the perilous Ploesti raid in August of 1943. The Ploesti raid was the famous low-level bombing mission where scores of B-24s flew from bases in Libya and attacked the German-held oil refinery in Ploesti, Romania. They flew in at tree top level and suffered heavy casualties where over 50 of the 177 planes and crews dispatched did not return to their bases. Buist later flew on the ill-fated Kassel mission raid with the 445th BG in September of 1944, where 25 out 30 B-24s from the 445th BG were shot down by the enemy. Both missions were the worst losses on single missions during the war. Buist may have the only USAAF claim to surviving both.

Jimmy Stewart flew in *Nine Yanks and a Jerk*

Nine Yanks and a Jerk was also flown by Jimmy Stewart on at least two missions. The first was when he led the 445th Bomb Group on a raid to bomb industrial targets at Frankfurt, Germany on January 29, 1944. He flew with Lt. Conley's crew (the crew he posed for a photo op with on p.40). One of the gunners on Conley's crew, S/Sgt. Harold Eckelberry, wrote in his diary on January 29th, *"Went to Frankfurt, Germany, today. Was a rough mission. Saw plenty of flack and lots of fighters. There was lots of flack over the target. Also plenty of M.E. 109s. Saw 12 in one bunch. Also had very good fighter support. Stewart flew as co-pilot. Got seven hours on this trip. Flew at 23,000 feet. 34 below zero."*

STEWART LEADS RAID ON FRANKFURT

Lt. Jack Heany, the bombardier on the Williams crew, flew as a replacement bombardier with a different crew on another plane that same day called *Mr. Smith* (probably named in honor of one of Jimmy Stewart's film characters, Jefferson Smith, from the movie *Mr. Smith Goes to Washington*). Jack was quoted in a debriefing report that day as saying, *"Fighter opposition against our group was nil. Our fighters were really on the ball. Flak was awfully heavy over the target."* The photo (above right), taken at Tibenham air base, appeared in the *Amsterdam Evening Recorder* newspaper in New York state for January 31, 1944. The caption below the picture read, *Major James Stewart (third from left), motion picture actor who now commands a Liberator bomber group in England, talks over a raid he led on Frankfurt, Germany, with three members of his crew of his Liberator "Nine Yanks and a Jerk." Left to right are: Lieut. John Rankin of Walhalia, S.C., Lieut. J.M. Steinhaven* [should be Steinhauser] *of River Forest, Ill., and Lieut. W.F. Conley of Greenville, Me. This photo was radioed from London to New York.*

Stewart went back to Frankfurt on February 4, 1944, on the same plane, but with a different crew. He flew

In a rare photo, Major James M. Stewart is shown in front of the control tower at Tibenham Airfield, England in February of 1944. The photo was taken not too long after he flew in *Nine Yanks and a Jerk*. He had just been promoted to the rank of Major at the end of January. This photo was taken by my father's fellow crew member and top turret gunner/flight engineer, T/Sgt. George Snook. George was stationed at Tibenham from November of 1943 through May of 1945. As Stewart had just exited the control tower, George asked the Major if he wouldn't mind posing for this candid shot. Stewart obliged him without any reservation. The men under Stewart's command said that Stewart was just like he is in the movies, a regular, down-to-earth guy, who didn't shirk his responsibilities. He flew some of the most dangerous combat missions as both squadron commander and group leader on many missions. My father and George said the men loved and respected him, and viewed him as a natural leader. George Snook said of him, "I flew with him several times. He was a prince of a guy. He wasn't an actor, but an excellent bomber pilot and a first rate officer. He was a pleasure to serve with." That was the sentiment of all the men who knew him. Photo courtesy of George Snook.

as co-pilot with Capt. Neil Johnson's crew in the lead plane, which was *Nine Yanks and a Jerk*. They were sent to bomb aviation industry and railroad yards targets in the Frankfurt area. Fortunately, they didn't experience any enemy aircraft encounters, but did see moderate to intense flak on the mission. The plane and crew returned to their base at Tibenham relatively unscathed. The Williams crew flew as his left wingman on that mission, flying their original plane #42-7580 – *"Hap" Hazard*.

Decals for *Nine Yanks and a Jerk*

Iliad Design has decals for a 1/72 B-24 model for *Nine Yanks and Jerk* in its *More Stars in the Sky* decals kit. Jimmy Stewart is featured at the top with this book's namesake. Clark Gable, Dan Rowan, and Ted Williams are also featured with the planes they flew combat in. Originally found online at http://www.iliad-esign.com/decals/72morestars.html.

Jimmy Stewart's WWII Military Service after the 445th Bomb Group

At the end of March of 1944, Stewart was transferred from the 445th Bomb Group. He was assigned to the 453rd Bomb Group (another B-24 Liberator group in the 2nd Combat Wing) to replace an operations officer who had been shot down. The men of the 445th were sorry to see him go. His promotion, however, was a natural progression within the Air Force. He had proven himself to be a competent leader and a skilled pilot in combat. His role in the 453rd was crucial in bringing up the poor morale at Old Buckenham (the 453rd's air base), which had been suffering due to heavy losses as well. Stewart was later promoted to an Operations Officer in the 2nd Combat Wing and eventually its Commander. He finished the war in Europe as a full bird colonel. It was said that if the war had gone on for six more months in Europe, Stewart would've been promoted to a general and/or possibly been made a group commander. He had risen in rank from a buck private to a full colonel in four years. It was quite an accomplishment. He had earned it, and was well-decorated for it, yet he was humble about his gallant service. His WWII decorations included the Distinguished Flying Cross with one Oak Leaf Cluster, the Air Medal with three Oak Leaf Clusters, and other medals, including the French Croix de Guerre with Palm. He is shown on the right receiving the French Croix de Guerre ('Cross of War') in January of 1945, from a representative of the French government for aiding in the liberation of France.

Nine Yanks and a Jerk flew its last mission (its 23rd one) on April 12, 1944, with 1st Lt. Samuel Schleichkorn's crew, which was a month and a half after the William's crew flew it. (Schleichkorn, who later changed his name to Gilbert Shawn after the war, will be referred as such below.) They flew in the #3 position, just to the left and slightly behind the lead plane, on a raid to Zwickau, Germany to attack

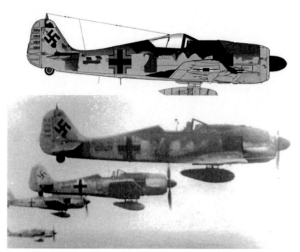

aircraft repair factories and a fighter airfield. *Nine Yanks and a Jerk* was flying as the left wingman to the lead ship flown by Capt. Neil Johnson, with the Williams crew flying to their right in the #2, deputy lead, position. The mission was recalled due to adverse weather over the target area and heavy vapor trails from the bombers' engines were obscuring visibility from about 10,000 to 20,000 feet. The code word, "Pepsodent!" was used to abort the mission and to get the bombers to turn around and head back home.

Staffelkapitän Oberleutnant Waldemar Radener's FW 190 A-7 WNr. 340 001 SV + DA 'Brown 4 + -' of 7./J.G. 26, Cambrai-Süd, France, May 1944 (T. Genth). From www.don-caldwell.we.bs/jg26/26kd2.htm and http://fw190.hobbyvista.com/genth1. htm.

Between 1:00 and 1:10 PM, after having just crossed the German border into Belgium, at an elevation of 17,000 feet, the group made its turn around to head back. Just then, about 50 to 60 gray and yellow-nosed FW 190s and ME 109s attacked the planes of the 445th Bomb Group from the 12 O'Clock high position. Their group was apparently singled out in the lead section of the 2nd Combat Wing formation, which was also leading the entire 2nd Air Division. Due to a lot of haze from about 10,000 feet to 25,000 feet, it was hard for the friendly fighters to see the beginning stages of the attack. A thin layer of stratus cloud had come between the 445th and its fighter escort. This gave the German fighters from three Staffeln (squadrons) in JG 26 and two from JG 2 an opportunity to attack the formation from beneath as well.[8] The Gerry fighters had formed over Juvincourt, France as a result of a German control center, Jahu 4, having correctly anticipated the bombers flight path. Once the B-24s' position had been determined, the enemy fighters were directed to Luxembourg. The bandits found the bomber stream and their large fighter escort near Liege, Belgium and began trailing them from there. Seizing the opportunity, the enemy fighters began to shoot their 20mm cannon shells

Photos of Radener from webpages http://www.luftwaffe.cz/radener.html and http://forum.axishistory.com/viewtopic.php?f=5&t=9174&p=77397.

right into the bellies of the thin-skinned Liberators. The most heavily attacked second section of the 445th Group's formation was 12 B-24s flying in the low left section, my father's section. As the group was over Liege, Belgium, they were getting strafed from all positions on the clock. The attacks lasted about 20 minutes as the bomber crews were left to defend themselves. Waldemar Radener led the German attacks.

---

8. JG stands for Jagdgeschwader, which is German for Fighter Wing. In this case the 26th and 2nd Fighter Wings.

Clock Positions around a Heavy Bomber

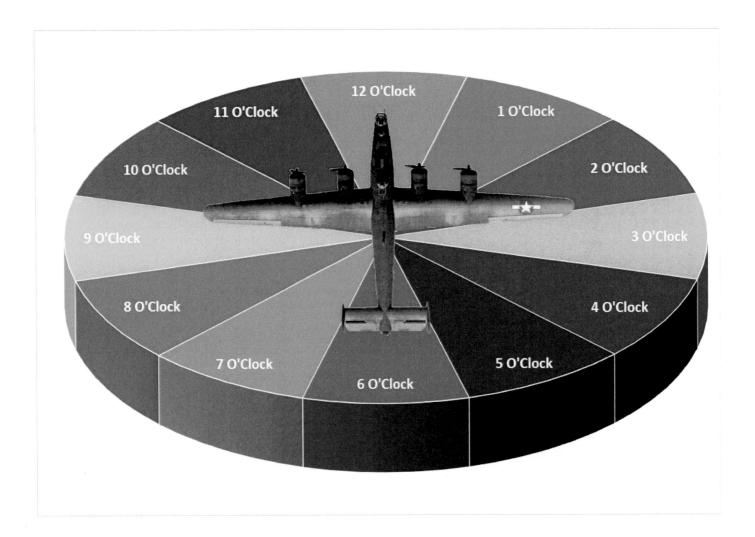

As enemy fighter planes (like the Me 109 below) attacked the heavy bombers, crew members called out the different positions around the clock that they came in from so that the gunners could fix their aim on the fast moving targets. For example, a fighter coming in from 12 O'Clock High was high above the bomber in the 12 O'Clock position. A fighter attacking from below at 6 O'Clock would be called out at "6 O'Clock Low." Many times the fighters would come at the bombers with the sun behind them so that the bomber crews would be blinded by the sun as the fighters dove in for the attack. Other times the enemy would come from below to shoot at the bombers' bellies. Coming in from several different positions was also a tactic used to throw the bombers' gunners into a panic and to distract their attention.

A German Me 109. Author's collection.

Distress calls went out to the Allied fighter escorts, who were nowhere to be seen in the bombers' moment of need because of the cloud formations which separated them. An emergency call had been put out for the Allied fighters to help. Well into the attack, American P-47 Thunderbolt fighters finally arrived. They chased the German fighters away, shooting down three of their new pilots. Sadly, it was too late for the crew of *Nine Yanks and a Jerk* and four other crews. The five bombers went down before the American fighters could come to their defense.

My father, S/Sgt. Hank Culver, was flying in the left waist gun position on the Williams' plane # 42-110041, *Lil' Nell*, in clear view of *Nine Yanks and a Jerk,* which was immediately to the left and literally only a stone's throw away. As the German fighter planes attacked, my father watched in horror as he saw *Nine Yanks and a Jerk* get strafed with incendiary bullets and 20mm cannon rounds from an FW-190 that set the plane on fire. The German fighter pilot who shot down *Nine Yanks and a Jerk* was Oberleutnant Waldemar Radener, Staffelkapitän (squadron commander) of Staffel (squadron) 7 of JG 26.[9]

The plane had two or three engines on fire with the mid-section also in flames. The right landing gear was also seen to be lowered. The electrical and hydraulics systems were also shot out. Several crew members were seen bailing out of the heavily damaged plane. From his left waist gun position my father saw the tail turret of *Nine Yanks and a Jerk* get shot off with the tail gunner, his friend Martin Clabaugh, trapped inside it and unable to escape.

Above: A P-47 Thunderbolt from the 56th Fighter Group flies close escort for a B-24. Left: The author in front of a P-47 on display at the American Air Museum at Duxford Airfield, England in July of 2013. These fighters, along with the P-51 Mustangs and P-38 Lightnings were referred to as "Little Friends" by the bomber crews. From http://www.littlefriends.co.uk/gallery, and author's collection.

9. It was Radener's 16th claim of an Allied plane.

As the gunner was going down, he gave my father a quick wave goodbye and all my father could do was return the wave as quickly as he could as he saw his friend drop to his death. Culver then watched the plane, which he had flown in only a month and a half before, go down in flames and explode upon impact. The rest of the crew managed to bail out. It was a terrible scene he never forgot. Many years later, in June of 2000, I interviewed him on video, and he remarked how that incident had really gotten to him at the time, and it was still obviously difficult to tell, even after 56 years.

There seems to be a conflicting report regarding the above incident. The ball turret gunner on *Nine Yanks and a Jerk*, S/Sgt. Robert Augustus, reported last seeing the tail gunner, Martin Clabaugh, stumble out of the tail gun turret and on fire just before he (Augustus) parachuted out of the plane as it was going into a dive. Augustus clearly recalled this many years later in a report for an Escape and Evasion journal. Augustus went on to say that he made an attempt to save his friend, but he was too on fire to rescue. The

The left waist gun position my father was at on his B-24 *Lil' Nell* when he saw *Nine Yanks and a Jerk* go down on April 12, 1944. This is not a photo of him, but one that shows a gunner's high altitude flight gear and gun position at the open window. Photo from http://www.8thafhs-pa.org/stories/bomb-group-gallery/44th-bomb-group/.

plane had just begun to nose down and spiral in, so Augustus bailed out in order to save himself. The stories appear to contradict one another. However, Augustus bailed out before he saw what finally happened to Clabaugh. It seems that the tail gunner must've returned to his position just before the turret was seen to be blown off. Several other crews reported seeing what Culver had witnessed. Lt. Sam Miller reported seeing the tail turret having been shot off as reported in his debriefing report after the mission. Miller's plane, #438, was flying a few planes to the left of *Nine Yank and a Jerk* as the scene unfolded. He reported the plane as having been shot down at 1:05 PM. Capt. Neil Johnson, flying in the lead position (which was slightly in front of *Nine Yanks and a Jerk*, and just to the right) reported seeing *Nine Yanks and a Jerk* get hit at approximately 1:13 PM. Some men on his crew, and perhaps Johnson himself, witnessed the tail turret having been shot off, apparently with the gunner still trapped inside it – *"tail turret shot off & tail gunner killed."*- was what his debriefing report said. Johnson remarked that the plane stayed with the formation in that condition for about 10 minutes and then spiraled down and crashed. Johnson saw several men bail out and their parachutes open during that time period. Lt. Edward Sadlon's and Lt. George Wright's crews also witnessed the tail turret having been shot off. Sadlon's and Wright's crews were flying behind *Nine Yanks and a Jerk* and just over to its right.

  Nine Yanks and a Jerk went down ablaze, and crashed in a field near Perwez, Belgium, having exploded when it crashed. All of the ill-fated plane's crew bailed out when the plane had gone down to about 6,000 to 7,000 in altitude, except the tail gunner. The radio operator, Fredrick Cotron, was KIA (Killed in Action) as a result of a broken neck when his parachute didn't open properly and he landed on a fence post. Shawn and four others evaded German capture for five months and secretly returned to England via the Belgium underground movement and the French Maquis (i.e. the French Underground and Resistance). Three other crew members were captured and became POWs (Prisoners of War), but were eventually repatriated as the

A B-24 on fire from the 44th BG photo collection. It is used here to illustrate how *Nine Yanks and a Jerk* suffered a similar fate. Photo from *NARA* and http://www.8thafhs-pa.org/stories/bomb-group-gallery/44th-bomb-group/.

Allied armies advanced through Belgium months later after D-Day. Four other 445th Bomb Group B-24s and their crews were also shot down that day. There are also memorials to them throughout Belgium.

  The Williams crew's radio operator, Frank Mangan, wrote the following in his diary for that mission - April 12, 1944: *"Up at 4:30. Went on mission to Zwickau, Germany. We got hell from fighters, our crew shot down 3, Bill & Snookie each got one. Am sure the Lord is with us."* Billy Fields, the left waist gunner (who shared that position with my father that day) reported in his debriefing report as follows: *Plane [an Me109] attacked flight from left and below from 7 O'Clock. I fired 50 rounds as he came close to us. He was on fire as he went into undercast.* My father, Hank Culver, may have gotten into the ball turret at this point, as some of the German fighters started coming in from lower positions. George Snook, the Williams crew's top turret gunner and flight engineer reported: *Five or six [Me109s] came in from high and 12 O'Clock. I picked out one who was firing at us and returned fire for about 50 or 60 rounds. Plane was in flames and passed over us.* The third fighter claim came from a stand-in gunner in the right waist gun position.

Ironically, on my father's plane that day was one of the original members of the *Nine Yanks and a Jerk* crew still left from the Metcalf crew – Stanley W. Treusch - who was flying combat missions as a replacement gunner. Treusch had not flown with his original crew on their fatal mission back on February 2nd when the crew went down in the North Sea, due to a case of frostbite he was recovering from on a previous mission. (James R. Crawford was another original crew member who was not on that crews' final mission. He had not yet come back from leave, and so he had also been spared from being a part of their demise. His status was unknown at this time.) Treusch, who was from New York City, was flying the right waist gun position on the Williams' plane *Lil' Nell* as a replacement for Henry Going who was not able to make that mission. It must've been another heartbreak for Treusch to see his original plane, the last memory of his original crew, go down in flames and crash that day. It was his original crew who named it and flew *Nine Yanks and a Jerk* to England from the States. While manning the right waist gun, Treusch reported having a probable German fighter claim according to the following debriefing report: *Plane [Me109] came in from 5 O'Clock and low. I fired about 70 rounds. He started smoking. His prop stopped and he went into overcast in a spin.* According to the Williams crew's reports above, there were at least a few consolations to the losses the 445th suffered that day with the enemy fighters they shot down. Treusch also went on to survive the war, and eventually retired to Florida.

In summary, the 445th put up a hell of a fight against their marauding attackers. The several waves of attacks by the German Me 109s and FW 190s fighters came in at 8-12 abreast, side by side, lined up for strafing runs on the formation from the typical 12 O'Clock High position to the 7 O'Clock to 5 O'Clock low positions. They figured if they could kill the tail gunners on the B-24s then they could close in for the kills on those aircraft. In less than 20 minutes, the German fighters had shot down the five B-24s from the 445th Bomb Group on that dreadful day. Several gunners on other B-24s had claimed additional enemy aircraft. Some gunners fired until they had used up their 500 rounds of ammunition, or until some of their guns had jammed. There would've been more claims if they hadn't run out of ammo or had the jammed guns. They were the only group, out of the 1st, 2nd, and 3rd Bomb Divisions' 455 plane raid, to lose any planes that day due to enemy aircraft encounters. It was a sore loss for the group again. Statistics like that didn't give much hope for an airman's life expectancy. The surviving crews that day had a lot to contemplate that evening as some huts were missing half of their members. It would be a reoccurring memory that would haunt them in the days, weeks, and months that followed.

What Happened on the Ground to the Last Crew that Flew *Nine Yanks and a Jerk*? What about the Remains of the Plane? The Incredible Story Continues…

My research into what finally happened to the squadron's famous plane led me to discover so much more than I had ever anticipated. It would lead me twice more to the European Continent, to visit the actual crash site in Belgium. I needed to see where my father's former plane found its final resting place, and to see what happened to the crew who last flew it, and where his friend Martin Clabaugh's body was interred for burial, or if it was recovered at all. I had also wondered if there were any surviving Belgians who were either at the site of the crash, or any who had knowledge of it and could explain it to me in detail. It was something I had to do in order to bring this unresolved part of my father's military service's story to a completion, and not to mention to satisfy my unending curiosity and growing fascination with his experiences and his fellow airmen's during the war. The story continued as follows, which was from a lead I got from a website host and new friends I met in Belgium, whom I will describe below.

After my father's crew witnessed the shoot down and descent of *Nine Yanks and a Jerk*, and saw Shawn's crew bail out (with the exception of the tail gunner, Martin Clabaugh), they always wondered what happened to that crew. The rest of the story on the ground is fascinating.

Most of Shawn's crew survived the parachute jump, with one exception - Fredrick Cotron. Cotron's parachute failed to open correctly as mentioned above. The pilot, Shawn (whose story we'll follow in detail), badly sprained his ankle and broke his leg upon impact with the ground, having landed in an orchard near

The Chateau at Maleves, Belgium as it looked in the 1940s where Louis Mandelaire worked as a grounds - keeper when he heard the crash of *Nine Yanks and a Jerk* about a mile away. Postcard photo courtesy of Rita (Mandelaire) Bombaerts.

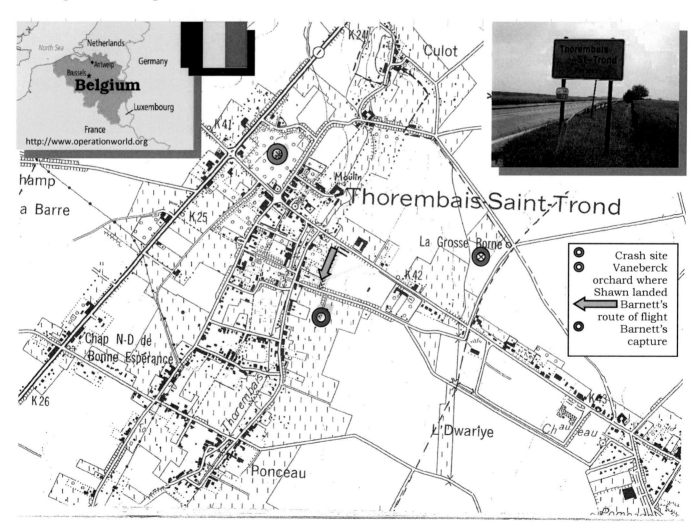

Large map and descriptions from notes by Benjamin Heylen, the museum curator of *Musée du Souvenir* in Maleves, Belgium. Benjamin gave me a copy of this to help illustrate the landing areas of a few of the last crew members as they bailed out near Perwez, Belgium. The crash site is about 30 miles southeast of Brussels.

the crash site. The rest of the crew members were scattered throughout the area.

In response to hearing the noise of the impact of the plane, a local farmer's 22 year old son, Louis Mandelaire, quickly jumped onto his bicycle and sped off to the site from a chateau in Maleves he was working at as a groundskeeper, which was about a mile from the crash site in Thorembais-Saint-Trond.

Being the first local person to arrive on the scene, Mandelaire beckoned to the downed pilot to come to him from the orchard he had landed in. Shawn, not only had hurt his right ankle in the jump, but also had his flight boots jolted off his feet from the initial jolt of the parachute as it opened. He limped about 100 yards over to him and was helped onto his bicycle, and was whisked off to another nearby village and hidden by other local Belgians. Mandelaire and the other Belgians risked their own lives in order to save Shawn's. Any Belgian caught harboring or trying to rescue an Allied flyer would be either shot or hung for treason by their German occupiers.

The German patrols quickly made their way to the crash site from the nearby town of Perwez (pronounced "Pear-way"), about a mile away, to see if they could capture the Americans alive. In spite of their attempts, Mandelaire's plan worked. He disappeared with Shawn before the Germans knew anything. He was able to get Shawn to a group in the Belgian resistance organization. One of the organization members, Mr. Francois Vandenberg, took and hid Shawn's parachute and harness. Mr. Vandenberg was later arrested by the Germans when they somehow discovered that he had hidden the chute.

Louis Mandelaire, shown here at age 20. Mandelaire rescued the downed pilot Gilbert Shawn from German capture by putting him on his bicycle and pedaling him off to safety to hide with the Belgian resistance. Courtesy Rita (Mandelaire) Bombaerts.

Because the plane had exploded upon impact, the crash had destroyed the Air Force's mission papers and flight instructions, which were secret and needed to be kept from falling into enemy hands. The local Belgians hid Shawn in a huge tree in a nearby forest for about 10 hours. While there, he soaked his ankle with wet maps to try to keep the swelling down. The Germans searched the woods, and even got as close as within 20 feet of him without detecting his whereabouts. Blood hounds had been used, but had lost the scent. At about 4:00 AM, Shawn was called out of the woods by being addressed as "President Roosevelt," by George Flabat (as Shawn's original name of Schleichkorn was too hard for the Belgians to remember and pronounce.) Shawn was then carried by three Belgians to a farm where arrangements were made to transport him to another location. Shawn carried an escape kit and brown purse with him as part of his Air Force escape equipment. When he was liberated months later, he reported in the Escape and Evasion report that he used the money to buy cigarettes, suspenders, and other items he needed. He also recalled how the lectures he had attended back in the States had helped him in this situation.

Shawn wound up staying with a George Flabat and his wife Rosa in the town of Orbais in the Brabant region of Belgium, which was about two and a half miles away from the crash site. Mr. Flabat was able to obtain civilian clothes from the resistance organization for Shawn to wear. (See below for the specifics of Shawn's escape and evasion over the following months.[10])

The crash site and memorial marker of the B-24 Liberator *Nine Yanks and a Jerk* and her last crew in Thorembais St. Trond, Belgium. The plane crashed at the far end of the green area to the right, beyond the rental car. The local farmer even plows up pieces of the wreckage after 70 years since the crash. The area is still agricultural like it was in 1944. Photo taken by author on July 7, 2014.

10. The specific details of Shawn's escape and evasion are chronicled as follows, according to his reports when he was liberated and interviewed by Allied forces.

After his time with the Flabats, Shawn was moved to the town of Gembloux (pronounced "Jom blue"), where he stayed with a Mrs. M. Peeters. While there, he had three doctors attend his foot and declared it fractured. He had his foot set by one of them, and remained there for three weeks, after which the FFI (the French Forces of the Interior resistance movement) moved him to Tourrine St. Lambert. He stayed in that area for two days with a Felix Quientin, and then eight days with a Mr. Arthur Hairson. After this he was moved by horse and buggy to stay with a Mr. and Mrs. Oscar Lenglez at 35 Rue de la Station in Perwez, Belgium. He was then moved back to Tourrine. While there, he spent three days a week with a Mr. Leon Bozart, who was the Chief of Police of Nil St. Vincent, in the Brabant region of Belgium. He was then driven to Namur by the organization, where he stayed eight days with a Mr. Louis Denis at 45 Rue de la Waterloo. From there he traveled to Charbon, Malone (Malpa) with Mr. Denis as a guide. He stayed with a Mr. Rene Denis who also housed two other aviators with him for eight days as well. After that he traveled via a bicycle with a guide. He changed guides twice while on his way to Beauvaing, Belgium. Shawn spent one night in a cabin and then moved on to Jehonville, in the Ardennes Forest, where he stayed in a camp. Shawn mentioned that a young Belgian was supplied with money from a London organization which helped to buy all of the food and supplies they needed. After nine days there, he and 23 other Allied airman were put up in a cabin in Porcheresse for about a month, where a Belgian provided them with food and money from the organization. A Madame Belley, of Dauerdisse, Belgium, also donated much food to the men.

A Mr. Emile Roiseux, of 81 Rue Livorno, Brussels, who was the chief of the organization, guided the aviators to Camp 3 near Bohan without incident. Shawn remarked how "we had excellent people helping us" there with food, equipment and other necessities. His report listed several Belgian individuals by name who were of great assistance to him and the others: Henri Maruis, of Bohan; Paul Henkart, of Bohan; Romain Héaux, of Bohan; Mr. Felix C. Becaquivor (Becquevort), of 90, Boulevard Saint Michel in Etterbeek, Brussels; René Delbart, 23, Rue Dansette, Jette; Mr. Jacques D. Bolle, 32 Rue de Florence, Brussels. He added that Madame "Buffuie" (most likely a Mrs. Alvina Bouffioux-Prevot, of 11 Rue Adolphe Damseaux), a seller of coal in Gembloux, was also a great help.

D. Deihl | R. Moreton | R. Morgan | K. Griesel | A. Roberts | D. Lloyd | A. Willis | H. Ashman G. Brenneke H. Gladys | G. Flather | G. Millar

Emile Roiseux

R. Weeden | C. Weymouth | M. Blakely | S. Schleichkorn R. Kindic | G Vogle | C. Mitchell | J. Evans | K. Doyle

Gilbert Shawn (Sam Schleichkorn) pictured above, kneeling fourth from the left. The photo, taken by Gaston Matthys, shows him and other Allied airmen who were brought to the camp in Porcheresse in August of 1944, a refuge of the Marathon transaction in which Allied airmen gathered in camps in the Belgian Ardennes and France. A special thanks to Regis Decobeck for this picture, as well as Marie-Claire-Roiseux-Vienne, daughter of Emile Roiseux for pictures of the house below.

Above and below taken from the website http://www.evasioncomete.org/fschleisg.html. Courtesy of Phillipe Connart.

The cabin/hut of the Hunters Camp Daverdisse used in August 1944. Hut in 1978 and 1984.

Samuel Schleichkorn's initials and last name are carved into the table that was at Camp Daverdisse in the Ardennes in Belgium among other Allied airmen who were hiding out with the Belgian Underground. The downed airmen named the table the "FESTIVE BOARD OF ALLIED AVIATORS." Photos courtesy of P. Connart and https://www.facebook.com/festiveboardofalliedaviators1944/timeline?ref=page_internal.

Photo reunion after the war - Extracted from "Maleves-Sainte-Marie-Wastines news - 1900-2000 "by Gerard and Gabriel Horion Pierard. http://www.evasioncomete.org/fschleisg.html

Shawn was eventually rescued by the advancing Allied armies in September of 1944, after spending four and half months evading capture. It is an incredible story of escape, evasion, and survival, especially considering that Shawn (whose original name was Samuel Schleichkorn) was Jewish. Had the Germans captured him, it would have been highly probable that he might not have survived the war. He was certainly indebted to the responsive, brave Belgians who came to his rescue. Shawn let his rescuers know that then, and by staying in contact with them throughout the decades since the war.

Many years after the war, Shawn returned a few times to the crash site and visited some of his Belgian friends who had rescued and assisted him. His last visit was in 2004, for the 60th anniversary of his bail out, escape and evasion. On April 10, 2004 (two days before the 70th anniversary of the mission), he took part as the honored guest for the dedication of the memorial marker of the crash of *Nine Yanks and a Jerk* in Thorembais St. Trond, near Perwez. At 83 years old, he attended the event at the crash site in memory of his fellow crew members.

He was given a box of parts of the plane found at the crash site over the years, which he took home with him to the United States. Shawn died the following year in Florida, where he had retired to. His story lives on today through his family, friends, and others who have an appreciation for his service, and that of his fellow airmen, who played a decisive role in the invasion and liberation of Nazi occupied Europe.

Me in a replica WWII U.S. Army Air Force dress uniform like my father's. I'm holding a photo of him on Omaha Beach, one of the American Landing Zones in Normandy, France on D-Day, June 6, 1944. Because of the efforts and sacrifices of the U.S. Army Air Forces, the Allied troops were able to land on these beaches (above) without being strafed by German aircraft. Yet, our troops landed under a hail of German ground gun fire and artillery shelling, which made this beach one of the bloodiest beaches during the invasion. Even so, the landing here led to the liberation of Nazi occupied Europe. Photo (L) taken on July 6, 2012, and *NARA*.

NINE YANKS AND A JERK AND AIRCREW MEMORIAL

A memorial marker is at the crash site today next to a field in Thorembais-Saint-Trond near Perwez, Belgium. *Nine Yanks and Jerk* crashed in the field near the marker shown in the picture below to the far left. The marker is written in French. It is translated as follows:

1944-2004

In recognition of all those who
contributed to the liberation of our villages
April 12, 1944 in the early afternoon,
upon return from a mission over Germany,
The B 24 H 41-29118 "Nine Yanks and Jerk" belonging to the
703rd Squadron of the 445th Bomb Group of the 8th American Air Force
crashed at this spot, shot down by the German fighters.

The members of the crew met different fates:

1st Lt. Gilbert S. Shawn	pilot	escaped
2nd Lt. James C. Barnett	co-pilot	prisoner
2nd Lt. Lloyd V. Hermanski	navigator	escaped
2nd Lt. Robert J. Pritchett	bombardier	escaped
T/Sgt. Raymond J. Ouellette	mechanic (engineer)	prisoner
T/Sgt. Fredrick J. Cotron	radio operator	killed
S/Sgt. Charles S. Bowman	front machine gunner	escaped
S/Sgt. Robert C. Augustus	ventral machine gunner	escaped
S/Sgt. Charles C. Harpin	side machine gunner	prisoner
S/Sgt. Martin E. Clabaugh	rear machine gunner	killed

Dedicated on April 10, 2004
in the presence of Lieutenant Colonel Gilbert S. Shawn, age 83 years old

The memorial marker for the last crew to fly *Nine Yanks and a Jerk* at Thorembais St. Trond, Belgium. The marker is near the field where the plane was shot down by German fighters. Lieutenant Colonel Gilbert S. Shawn was present for its dedication on April 10, 2004. Photo taken by the author on July 7, 2014.

1944-2004

Reconnaissance à tous ceux qui
ont contribué à la libération de nos villages

Le 12 avril 1944 en début d'après-midi,
de retour de mission au-dessus de l'Allemagne,
le B 24 H 41-29118 « Nine yanks and a jerk » appartenant au
703ᵉ escadron du 445ᵉ groupe de bombardiers de la 8ᵉ armée de l'air américaine
s'écrasa à cet endroit, abattu par la chasse allemande.

Les membres de l'équipage connurent des destins divers :

1ˢᵗ Lt. Gilbert S. Shawn	pilote	évadé
2ⁿᵈ Lt. James C. Barnett	copilote	prisonnier
2ⁿᵈ Lt. Lloyd V. Hermanski	navigateur	évadé
2ⁿᵈ Lt. Robert J. Pritchett	bombardier	évadé
T/Sgt. Raymond J. Ouellette	mécanicien	prisonnier
T/Sgt. Frederick J. Cotron	opérateur radio	tué
S/Sgt. Charles S. Bowman	mitrailleur avant	évadé
S/Sgt. Robert C. Augustus	mitrailleur ventral	évadé
S/Sgt. Charles C. Harpin	mitrailleur latéral	prisonnier
S/Sgt. Martin E. Clabaugh	mitrailleur arrière	tué

Inauguré le 10 avril 2004
en présence du lieutenant-colonel Gilbert S. Shawn, âgé de 83 ans.

The names of Shawn's crew are inscribed on the memorial marker along with a brief description of the mission, the crash, and their individual notations of the crew members having been killed in action and their evasions and captures. Notice the tail markings reflect the 445th Bomb Group's newer markings, which were painted on at the end of March of 1944. The white circle with the black "F" had been replaced with a black background with a white horizontal stripe. The 703rd Bomb Squadron patch logo can be seen on the right of the marker. Photos of the marker taken by the author on July 7, 2014.

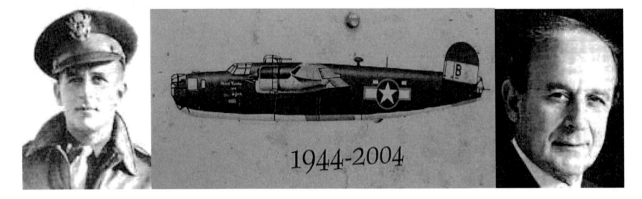

1944-2004

Gilbert Shawn, the pilot of *Nine Yanks and Jerk* on its final mission, evaded capture for close to five months and was repatriated via the Belgium underground movement. Shawn returned to the crash site in Belgium 60 years later to be there for the dedication ceremony of the memorial marker.

Photos of Shawn are taken from the book, "Air Forces Escape & Evasion Society," published in 1992 by Turner Publishing Company, Paducah, KY, and the website http://www.evasioncomete.org/fschleisg.html 2012.

MY FIRST VISIT TO THE CRASH SITE OF *NINE YANKS AND A JERK*

On July 8, 2014 (as a result of an internet connection during the previous months with a mutual friend Eduoard Renoire), I was directed to visit the crash site and meet with Louis Mandelaire's daughter Rita Bombaerts and her husband Fred (pictured on the next page), along with a couple of their friends. Late that morning, the Bombaerts, Josianne Flabat, Christian Barbier and I had tea and coffee at a local café where I interviewed all of them for about two hours. Rita was so excited to share her father's story with me and to have me share it with our present and future generations. Rita, who speaks French, was translated through her husband Fred. She told me about how her father heard the crash of *Nine Yanks and a Jerk* and immediately hopped on his bicycle and sped off to see if he could reach any of the downed airmen. As mentioned above, he had biked about a mile from the grounds he was working on. His diligence paid off. When he saw the pilot, who had landed a few hundred yards from the plane's wreckage, he motioned to Shawn to come away from the orchard he had landed in and to get onto his bike. Mandelaire was able to get Shawn away from the area quickly enough so that the German patrols never caught up with them. Louis had risked his own life to save an American airman's life. He was returning the favor. Rita mentioned how her father was part of the Belgian underground, yet he rarely had spoken of his activities to her and her family, even after many years since the war. She did, however, manage to hear this much of the above story from him.

Rita went on to tell me how her mother's parents' home was destroyed by German artillery during the initial take-over of the area by the Germans. When the war was over and they eventually returned to their home, they had found some spent brass German shell casings in the rubble of the house. Her mother polished them up and eventually displayed them on their mantle over the fireplace once their home was rebuilt. Rita gave me two of them to keep as souvenirs and tokens of our time together. It was a very kind and gracious gesture on her part. I made a few more friends for life in my European travels, as I've retraced my father's footsteps and flight paths.

In the late afternoon and early evening of the same day, I met Benjamin Heylen, a local museum curator, at the crash site. While there, we posed for a photo at the memorial (see below). Due to the rain, we quickly left the site. We then visited his fantastic WWII museum, *Musée du Souvenir*, a few miles away in Maleves. Benjamin has been collecting real Allied and German WWII uniforms, weapons, supplies, and memorabilia most of his life. He has it housed in his grandfather's former barn (now remodeled), where it is well-presented and secured. It is a must-see attraction which displays the region's WWII history quite thoroughly.

Photo of Fox News broadcaster Eric Shawn, Gilbert Shawn's son. From http://www.foxnews.com/on/personalities/ericshawn/bio

Benjamin and his brother also took me through their local village to show me the various places where Gilbert Shawn was hidden until the Americans arrived several months after D-Day. Shawn had been moved back and forth between several residences and properties during his five months of escape and evasion. Benjamin's own grandfather was part of the Belgian underground and had helped other airmen escape and evade capture as well.

The museum is quite a tribute to the Allies whom his family had helped, and to the Belgians who risked their own lives during the German occupation of their country. These Belgian descendants of that WWII generation have a great appreciation for the Allies and their Belgian counterparts who helped the Allies during those dark days in WWII, some 70 years ago.

Another incredible twist to this story is what I came to learn from Benjamin himself, and much to my surprise. Gilbert Shawn's son is Eric Shawn, one of Fox News' commentators. I've seen Eric on Fox News many times over the years in the States, but never made the connection. Benjamin later helped put me in touch with Eric. After my trip to Belgium (thanks to Benjamin), Eric and I have since corresponded. We were both amazed at how small a world it is that we live in. We wrote to each other about how our fathers served in the same squadron and flight formation during the war, and under Jimmy Stewart's

On July 8, 2014, Fred and Rita (Mandelaire) Bombaerts and I met at the crash site memorial. It was a typical rainy day in Belgium. It was Rita's father who initially rescued Gilbert Shawn. Freddy had worked in the United States many years ago and was able to translate between English and French for my interview with him and Rita and their friends. We spent the next two hours in a local café. Rita also showed me her father's gravesite in nearby Perwez. We stopped there to pay our respects to her father, who risked his life to save Gilbert Shawn's. It was a moving experience for us both. I also felt like I had finally pieced together a fuller picture of my father's WWII service. Being able to stand at these sites, after hearing my father's WWII stories growing up, made the picture come to life. It was as much a blessing for Rita and Freddy as it was for me. We continue to correspond with one another. I've made new friends for life as a result.

command. We also reflected upon how my father witnessed his father's plane get shot down and the crew's bailout. Eric encouraged me to continue to tell the story. He also reminded me of how he has lived the story growing up with his father and had heard his dad tell it to him many times, much like my father and me. He remarked on how much he and his wife and son enjoyed their trip to Belgium, just weeks after I had visited the various places and people mentioned above. I shared the same sentiment with him. Our new Belgian friends are wonderful hosts who truly appreciate what the Americans did for their liberties.

The author and Benjamin Heylen, a local WWII Museum curator who explained from the ground perspective the crash of *Nine Yanks and Jerk* and what followed. Benjamin was kind enough to give me a small piece of the wreckage that was recovered by the local farmer whose property still yields pieces of the crashed plane when he plows his field. July 8, 2014. Author's collection.

Me at Benjamin's *Musee de Souvenir* in Maleves, Belgium. I'm holding a piece of the wreckage of *Nine Yanks and a Jerk* – a spent .50 caliber machine gun bullet casing – the same type my father fired from his waist gun position on the same plane.

July 8, 2014.

MY SECOND VISIT TO THE CRASH SITE IN 2015, AND AN INCREDIBLE DISCOVERY

The author looking out across the field in Thorembais St. Trond, Belgium where *Nine Yanks and a Jerk* crashed on April 12, 1944. This photo was taken the day after the events described below. Author's collection.

On June 25, 2015, I picked up my rental car at Charles de Gaulle Airport in Paris, France and sped off at about 6:30 AM, just before a major taxi cab drivers' strike blocked the highways and airport exits. (I took a cab from my hotel in Paris at 5:00 AM to get to the airport to avoid the strike.) I then drove three hours and forty minutes to Perwez, Belgium near the crash site of *Nine Yanks and a Jerk*. I arrived in the area late in the morning. Because I had arrived too early to go to my bed and breakfast hostel, I ate brunch at a local café, Afterward, I drove about a mile to the crash site in Thorembais St. Trond. I took advantage of the great weather and shot a few still photos of the memorial marker, the farm where the crash

Vapor trails still line the skies over central Belgium as they did in WWII. Photo taken on June 25, 2015. Author's collection.

site was, and even took a few photos of the blue skies with vapor trails which marked the paths of current commercial planes high above me. The distinct white trails in the skies reminded me of how Belgium was said to be the 'bomber autobahn" or "bomber highway" between the 8th Air Force bomber bases in England and their targets in Germany during WWII. The present-day vapor trails even show similar flight patterns. During the war there would've been many more white trails in the sky than what I was witnessing on this clear morning.

After spending a half an hour taking a series of photos in the beautiful weather, which was about 75^{0}F (24^{0}C) with a cool breeze and mostly sunny skies, I turned my rental car around to go back down the narrow farm road I came in by. Just then I saw a wonderful sight.

As I just turned around and was passing by the memorial marker, a beautiful blonde woman came riding up on horseback across the farm toward my car. It was like a scene out of a movie. I quickly brought the car to a stop and lowered the passenger side window to ask her a couple of questions. I initially asked, "Pardone madame, parle vous Englis?" She immediately replied, "Yes, a little bit." I then proceeded to ask her if she knew who the local farmer was who owned the property. I explained how I'm writing a book about my father's WWII service and that a plane he had once flown in was shot down with another crew in it, and how it had crashed at this site in WWII. I explained that he was flying next to it when it went down. I also explained that I was hoping to find any pieces of the wreckage that the farm owner might still be plowing up.

Lauretta led me down the narrow path from the memorial site over to the farm owner's stables with the two dogs and me in trail. June 25, 2015. I took the photo from my car as I felt like I was living a movie scene.

She explained in good English, with her French accent, that her horses were stabled at the owner's barns just across the field from where we were talking. She told me to follow her down the paved path to the owner's barns and we could then talk with him. So, I turned my car around and followed her in my rental as she galloped ahead on the horse down the narrow road, with two dogs following her. I felt like I was in a movie scene. I was amazed.

She led me to the stable, where I parked my car. I then introduced myself to her and the farm owner. She told me that her name is Lauretta. The farm owner introduced himself (whose name escapes me now). He spoke very good English as well. I explained to him my mission. I also gave him a copy of my business card with my contact information. The farm owner told me that no parts of the plane had been plowed up very recently, but if he came across any he would be sure to e-mail me and let me know. He did say, however, that just down the road a few houses from here lives a man, 89 year old Marcel Barras, who was an eyewitness to the bail outs of the crew and the crash of the plane. I was stunned! So was Lauretta. The farmer said that we could walk to his house, which was a stone's throw away.

So, the three of us walked down the street called Rue du Culot. At the bend in the road is Marcel's home. Lauretta knocked on the door. Much to our surprise he opened it and greeted us. He seemed as shocked as we were. Marcel has lived in the same home since the crash of *Nine Yanks and a Jerk*. It was his boyhood home. Lauretta began translating my questions as I explained to him why I was there and what I hoped to learn from him about the bail outs of the crew and how he saw the plane go down just about a half a mile from his front door. He stepped outside and began to converse with us. Having Lauretta as an interpreter was a gift for me that day. The farmer also translated for me a little bit as well. I quickly turned on my video camera to record our conversation. Marcel was our incredible discovery.

Marcel's story is as follows. He was about 18 years old when he witnessed the events of April 12, 1944. He worked near the crash site because he was a farmer assisting his father in cultivating the land. As the events of that day unfolded, he was inside the house when his mother or sister had told him that they heard a plane in trouble and that it was going down. He rushed outside to see what was happening. As he looked up into the sky, Marcel saw all of the crew members (except, of course, Martin Clabaugh) jump out of the plane. He saw all of the chutes open, except one. Marcel witnessed the radio operator T/Sgt. Fred Cotron's death when his chute did not open. Cotron was killed upon impact as he landed on a fence post nearby. As the rest hit the ground, many of them were quickly taken by the local Belgian resistance movement to the village of Maleves in order to hide them from the German patrols that were fast approaching from two different villages in opposite directions. He watched as the pilot, Gilbert Shawn, banked the plane in a large turn, away from the nearby village of Orbais, so that it wouldn't kill any villagers. Shawn stayed with the plane until it was at a very low altitude and he felt it was clear of the village, and then bailed out while he still had enough altitude for his chute to open. Marcel watched it all. He said that some of the Americans were hidden in a castle at Maleves and at various other places until some of them were repatriated when the American army came through the area in September of 1944.

Marcel Barras, at age 89, still stands straight as an arrow and was very sharp and clear in his description of the events that happened 71 years ago. He had Lauretta laughing during our photo shoot. June 25, 2015. Author's collection.

I asked him if he knew if any pieces of the plane might still exist as souvenirs taken by the locals

Perwez municipal building.

at that time. He said that he did not know of any. The remains of the plane were eventually taken on a German truck and scrapped. Some of the local villagers, however, had taken pieces of the plexiglass and made rings from them as souvenirs, but the whereabouts of those items is long forgotten. It was astounding to hear him tell the story like it happened yesterday. He was passionate and full of vigor in his telling of it.

I believe that he enjoyed our company as much as we enjoyed his for those few minutes we spent together. Our meeting was the highlight of my entire European trip this year. What a discovery! It was an incredible experience all around. I thanked Marcel for his time and let him know that it was a real pleasure to meet him.

As we walked back to the stables, Lauretta suggested that I contact the municipal building in Perwez to see if I could find anything more about the crash and what happened to the plane and crew. She looked up the address on her IPhone and wrote it down for me. They were open late that evening, so I could go and investigate through them a little more, which I did later. Although they had nothing in the office to show me, it turned out that they wound up contacting Benjamin Heylen. I laughed when they told me who they were calling, because he was my contact from last year, and I was scheduled to go on a tour of Bastogne with him and his family and friends on Saturday. He and I spoke on the phone briefly about my research and our meeting on Saturday. It turned out that his brother works in the municipal office, so he had exhausted all research there already.

When Lauretta and I got back to the stables, she took me next door where I met a few other locals whom she introduced me to. Some of them said that they have some relatives who now live in the United States who might have some photos of this area from WWII, and possibly one of the plane at the crash site. They said that they would contact them and see if they could track down any photos that I might be interested in. I gave them my business card with my contact information. I continue to look forward to what might yet be revealed concerning this plane and its crews' histories.

After a few minutes of conversation, I then said my goodbyes to them and Lauretta and thanked them all for their help. I had asked Lauretta earlier what she did for a living. Talk about a connection with aviation – she told me that she is a commercial airline pilot for Brussels Airlines.[11] I was quite impressed. She told me that she flies to New York about once a month. I told her that if she ever flies into New York, I'd be glad to buy her dinner for helping me out this day. I told her what a blessing she was to me in all that she did, and that was the least that I could do. She said that she would like that. I gave her my business card. It was great to meet someone of her background who appreciates what I've been doing.

A couple of days later, I paid a visit to Fred and Rita Bombaerts in Gembloux. I shared the above story with them. Much to my surprise (again), Marcel's late wife was the cousin of Rita's mother. So, they have known each other since Rita's childhood. We all got a laugh after we made the connections. When I got back to the U.S., I sent them copies of the photos I took of Marcel and Lauretta that day. Rita and Fred have since contacted Marcel and discussed our unique meeting. We hope to obtain a copy of a photo of Marcel when he was 18 years old, at the time of the crash, to be included in *Daylight Raiders*.

A panoramic view of the farmer's field where *Nine Yanks and a Jerk* crashed.
The town of Perwez is in the distance. Photo taken on June 25, 2015. Author's collection.

11. I later found out that she piloted, as Captain, the first all-female crew on Brussels Airlines Airbus 300 from Brussels to New York in March of 2014. She has worked for the airlines for 17 years. See the following link, http://press.brusselsairlines.com/100-female-brussels-airlines-crew-flies-to-new-york-on-international-womens-day.

CLOSURE

IN MEMORY OF STAFF SERGEANT MARTIN CLABAUGH
AND THOSE WHO NEVER RETURNED

My second trip also brought closure to a part of this story and journey that I had heard growing up in the 45 years I had my father with me. It answered a few questions I had. What happened to Martin Clabaugh's body? Was it ever recovered? Was there a final resting place for my father's friend? I had one last stop to make on my four day trip to Belgium. It was on Sunday, June 28, 2015.

The day before, on Saturday, Benjamin Heylen and his family and friends had taken me on a fantastic personal tour of Bastogne, the areas the Battle of the Bulge had been fought in throughout southern Belgium, and to several museums (not to mention a couple of good Belgian restaurants as well). While on the tour, I asked Benjamin what he personally knew about the tail gunner's body – was it ever recovered? Was there a burial and final resting place for him? Benjamin, who has an excellent knowledge of the crew and their story, sadly replied, "The body was never recovered. However, he is memorialized at the American Cemetery at Henri-Chapelle in Belgium." It was about an hour and fifteen minute drive from my bed and breakfast lodging in Aische en Refail near Perwez. The cemetery and memorial are about 70 miles southeast of Brussels.

It was late Sunday morning, as I drove down the E42 to the A3 and then onto the N3 to Henri-Chapelle. I was dressed in an original WWII U.S. Army Air Force dress uniform with the patches, rank, and ribbons made to look like my father's, and Martin Clabaugh's. I wanted to dress in honor of my father's combat buddy and to pay my respects to all of the men who served and died for our freedoms. As I looked at the beautiful Belgian countryside and the green farms from my car, a thought occurred to me - the last person Martin Clabaugh saw before his death was my father. I recalled how my father had said that when the tail turret was shot off *Nine Yanks and a Jerk*, Clabaugh gave my father a quick wave goodbye as he went down in the turret. All my father could do was return his wave with a quick one also.

That's all they both had time for. Just like that, his friend was gone. With my newly discovered information, it seemed befitting (since my father never knew what finally happened to his friend) that I would go and pay my respects by visiting the memorial to him, and so complete the story I had set out to write. I was all the more determined to go there. I fixed my gaze ahead and looked for the exit to Henri-Chapelle.

After exiting the A3, I followed the country road a few miles along a picturesque ridgeline and took in the majestic sight of the green farms sweeping through the valley below on my way to the village of Henri-Chapelle. As I turned left just before entering the centuries old village, I saw a traffic circle where I noticed a large crucifix in the circle near my turn. It was typical of many French and Belgian villages – a sign of the local faith that has played an active role in the region for centuries. I made the left on to the Rue de Memorial Americain (i.e. the road to the American Memorial) Again, I saw the valley below between the two ridges, only from a different angle – it was a scene like a painting. It was like gazing upon emerald green carpeting, with all other shades of green, rolling down the slopes into the valley. The green farms reminded me of why the medal and ribbon for the European-African-Middle Eastern campaign (above) has the green stripes on it. They are on it to symbolize the green fields of Europe for those who served there in the U.S. military. It is quite befitting.

Above: One of my first views of the cemetery and memorial property. Behind me is the lush green valley that the American Cemetery and Memorial at Henri-Chapelle overlooks. It was a place of somber reflection regarding the costs of our freedoms and the liberation of Europe. Many of our men fought, bled, and died in this valley and on this ridge during the campaign to fight our way to Germany. Below: The front view of the American Memorial at Henri-Chapelle. The cemetery is behind it. Photos taken on June 28, 2015.

The beautiful flower garden in front of the American Cemetery and Memorial at Henri-Chapelle, Belgium. I took a few shots here to show how beautifully the gardens and grounds are kept. The Superintendent of the monument is in the golf cart in the background in front of the Wall of Remembrance. June 28, 2015.

The cemetery sits on a beautiful ridge, opposite the one I drove in on, that overlooks the lush green hills and valleys the Americans fought their way through during the Battle of the Bulge and the press toward Germany. In contrast, I also saw some of the old, gray cement German bunkers, like signs of death, still in their emplacements next to the road overlooking the valley that was full of life below. I thought of how our men had to face these guns and eventually capture them. How many of our men died or were wounded before that happened? They were silent reminders of the costs involved for our freedoms. The cemetery was also not too far from the German border. The first German city to fall to the Allies was Aachen, which was only about 12 miles away - just about a half hour drive.

I found the parking area, parked my rental car, walked about fifty yards from my parking spot, and then looked out across the ridge and the valley below. I paused to reflect upon the journey our troops had made across northern France, Belgium, Luxembourg, and Holland with the U.S. First Army from D-Day, June 6, 1944 until they got into this area in September and October of 1944. The battles fought through these areas, and the Huertgen Forest, raged from that time through the early spring of 1945. I thought about the enemy armies they faced on these hills and valleys. Many of the men buried here were also in the Battle of the Bulge in December of 1944, as it was Germany's last push back at the Allied advance in the Ardennes. I thought about my uncle, Capt. Louis Muhlbauer, who had served with the U.S. Army here, and lived to tell about it. I stood there thinking about what it cost our nation in terms of men's lives and the American blood that was shed across the beautiful, panoramic vista I was looking out over. It was hard to believe it was once a battlefield. I thought to myself, "Every American who could afford a trip here should come to see what our guys had to go through in order to liberate Europe and keep the world free." It was too much to take in at once. I looked out across the valley for quite a while from the different angles.

I made sure that I took adequate time to soak in the landscape. After some time of reflection upon the scene, I set up my camera to take a few memorable photos of the ridge and the valley below. I wanted people back home in the U.S., and my friends in Europe, to get a glimpse of what our soldiers had to face and endure in those vexing months of World War II. I then made my way over to the cemetery.

As I made my way across the path from the ridge to the cemetery, there were crowds of motorcycle and moped riders gathering for some sort of an organized ride. As I crossed the street, I saw the Superintendent of the cemetery in his golf cart keeping an eye on things. I decided to take a photo of myself in front of the bright red flower garden out front to show how beautifully kept the gardens and grounds are. The Superintendent was watching me as I stood for the timed shots. After a couple of shots, I made my way over to greet the man, and introduced myself to him. He asked why I was dressed in a WWII U.S. Army Air Force uniform. At first he thought that I was a European re-enactor dressed as an American airman. I explained to him how I was retracing my father's footsteps and flight paths for the book I'm writing, *Daylight Raiders*. I explained that the book is about his entire life, but especially his WWII service. I explained to him that I'm from New Jersey, but not to hold that against me. We got a

A view of about half of the nearly 8,000 American graves at Henri-Chapelle Cemetery. Like my previous visits to the American cemeteries at Colleville at Omaha Beach in Normandy, France and at Maddingly near Cambridge, England, this was also a deeply moving experience. Seeing the loss of American life here was heart-breaking. I thought of all of these young men in their late teens and twenties killed in action, in the prime of life, for our freedoms. My father always said that the real heroes were the ones who never made it home. I couldn't agree more.

chuckle out of it. I then went on to explain how I also came to pay my respects to his combat buddy, Martin Clabaugh. I explained the sad tale about S/Sgt. Clabaugh to him. He introduced himself as Alvin Nagel, also an American. Alvin commended me for what I was doing, and was all too glad to direct me to the visitor's map room just behind us so that I could locate the memorial recorded in a ledger there.

I opened the heavy bronze door to the map room, walked inside, and saw the research ledger on the table. I also saw two huge wall maps of the Battle of the Bulge and the American advance into Germany, The vast amount of men involved on both sides was incredible to contemplate. It was a lot to digest. I took a few minutes to study them. After that, I read some of the descriptive panels. I took a few photos of the room to take home to look at in more detail. I signed the guest register, and noted what a beautifully kept site it is. I then looked through the cemetery's ledger that had all of the men's names who were either buried there, or memorialized on the Wall of Remembrance. I confirmed through the ledger

"The bronze statue of the Angel of Peace is bestowing the olive branch upon the heroic dead for whom he makes special commendation to the Almighty." From the American Battle Monuments Commission brochure.

that there was indeed no grave site for Martin. As Benjamin had said, the body was never recovered by the Americans. I did see that he was in fact memorialized on the wall just a few paces outside the room I was in.

The Wall of Remembrance has a colonnade with several panels separated from each other under a roof covering. I had to look on both sides of each panel to find his name. The names of the memorialized were in alphabetical order by last name. Seeing that the sky looked a bit overcast, with a possible shower in the near future, I decided to walk through the cemetery first, before the chance of rain, and then come back to Martin Clabaugh's wall panel. I figured if it did rain I could always come back under the roof for cover and see his name inscribed on the wall.

I descended the staircase outside. The steps are designed to be long and wide to break one's stride as one enters the cemetery grounds. They are also in a large diamond shape with half to the left, the rest on the right All of this is to keep visitors from rushing down the steps, but rather to inspire pause and reflection upon the view in front of them of the thousands upon thousands of the American war dead.

I slowly walked through the rows of nearly 8,000 graves. I paused at some of the names I recognized from my studies of the war and what I quickly read in the map room.[12] The scene was a striking reminder of how many Americans died in these areas. I paused for some reflection and prayer at some of the grave sites. I thanked God for these brave men and what they did for our freedoms and for the liberation of Europe. I also prayed for the repose of their souls. It was heart-breaking to see all of those white Latin Crosses and Stars of David before me. I made sure that I took plenty of photos and video to show both Americans and Europeans just what the cost of freedom was here. Words alone could not express the sense of loss of life, the families that were never realized, and the American sons who never returned.

I learned that from Benjamin and Alvin that Belgian school children are brought to this cemetery, and other American cemeteries in the region, to learn the prices of their freedom. It's a lesson we in the U.S. could learn to do as well with our children.[13]

After my tour of the cemetery, I returned to the Wall of Remembrance and found Martin's name. Each panel has a state name at the top to recognize each state of the United States. Martin's name was under the panel with Georgia at the top. Although he and the other men listed on that panel were not necessarily from that state (as he was from Ohio), this is how the memorial is set up.

I took the time to reflect upon the final moments of this man's life and recalled what my father had told me about this brave soul. Looking at his name and thinking about his sacrifice in WWII was deeply moving to me. It also brought closure to the story I had heard my father tell all of my life. I finally felt that my mission here had been completed. As mentioned earlier, my father always said that the real heroes were the ones who never came back, meaning those who died in the war. Martin Clabaugh was one

---

12. I walked through the cemetery and photographed some familiar names of airmen on the grave markers. Some notable men who are buried at the cemetery are the namesakes of some of our Air Force bases in the U.S. The former, now closed, Castle AFB near Merced, California was named in honor of Brigadier General W. Fredrick Castle who died at the controls of his B-17 while it was going down in flames on Christmas Eve in 1944. Castle stayed at the controls until all of his crew bailed, but the plane exploded before he could escape himself. Castle AFB became a major SAC (Strategic Air Command) base during the Cold War era. Castle was posthumously awarded the Medal of Honor for his self-sacrifice. Nellis AFB near Las Vegas, Nevada was named in honor of Lt. William H. Nellis, a native of Las Vegas, who was shot down in his P-47 Thunderbolt during the Battle of the Bulge on December 27, 1944. While strafing a German convoy in Luxembourg, his plane was shot down by ground fire. Being too low to bail out, he was killed in the crash of the plane. His remains were recovered the following April in 1945 and he was buried at Henri-Chapelle that year. Other soldiers buried there who won the Medal of Honor are Pfc. Francis X. McGraw and Tec 4 Truman Kimbro. See website for more information at https://www.abmc.gov/cemeteries-memorials/europe/henri-chapelle-american-cemetery.

13. When I was a school teacher, I taught fifth grade American History and sixth grade World History. I always made sure that my students knew something about the costs for our freedoms. Each year I taught lessons about our military holidays and significant anniversary dates in my classes, especially as they related to WWII, other wars, and our current military. I taught them about Veterans Day, Pearl Harbor Day, Armed Forces Day, Memorial Day, VE and VJ Days, and D-Day. In the last few years, after I had acquired real and replica WWII uniforms, I wore them on many of the above mentioned holidays and dates to illustrate and make the lessons more tangible. I also wore my U.S. Air Force uniforms from the era I was in during the 1980s. I showed slides of my travels too. Hopefully it made an impression upon the hundreds of 10-12 year olds I taught over a twenty year period.

The colonnade at Henri-Chapelle Cemetery and Memorial. Staff Sergeant Martin Clabaugh's name was etched in the marble panel under the State of Georgia (on the left). His name is among the 450 Americans listed as missing. The memorial chapel is at the end of the colonnade. Below: Inside the memorial chapel. The words on the altar read: I GIVE UNTO THEM ETERNAL LIFE AND THEY SHALL NEVER PERISH.

of the many who gave his life in the service of our country and Europe's liberation. I took several photos and shot a couple of video segments with narration in front of his name. I wanted to keep this for posterity and to one day share with a larger audience. One of the themes that ran through my mind once again is what I always tried to drill into my students' minds when I was a school teacher – FREEDOM IS NEVER FREE – thousands of our men and women paid for it with their lives. As the military saying goes, All Gave Some, Some Gave All. Amen.

As I looked at Martin E. Clabaugh's name etched in stone, I remembered my father's heartfelt words to me about this man's final moments on April 12, 1944. Viewing his name and reflecting upon my father's words was quite a memorable experience. It was a privilege and an honor to be at this site in remembrance of his sacrifice in WWII. I wore the French Croix de Guerre (Cross of War) medal, which the 445 BG was awarded.

Left: The panel at the beginning of the colonnade reads as follows:

HERE ARE RECORDED

THE NAMES OF AMERICANS

WHO GAVE THEIR LIVES

IN THE SERVICE

OF THEIR COUNTRY

AND WHO SLEEP

IN UKNOWN GRAVES

Above: The words at the beginning of the colonnade honoring the sacrifices of our men buried and memorialized here. Below: Looking across the multitude of crosses where many of our fallen airmen and soldiers found their final resting places. Every American cemetery in Europe is immaculately kept.

Above: The rows of graves marked by the numerous crosses with the Wall of Remembrance colonnade in the background. Below: (L) The grave of Medal of Honor recipient Brigadier General Fredrick W. Castle. (R) The grave of Lt. William H. Nellis. Two U.S. Air Force bases were named in honor of these fallen airmen.

Nine Yanks and a Jerk

B-24H Liberator   Serial Number 41-29118

Manufactured by Consolidated/Forth Worth

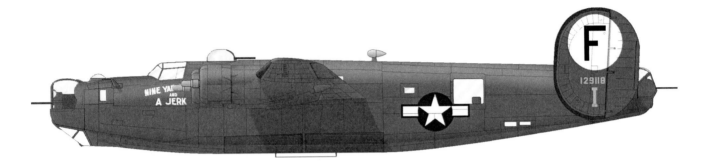

U.S. Eighth Air Force

445th Bomb Group

703rd Bomb Squadron

445th Bomb Group logo courtesy of 2nd Air Division Association and Mike Simpson 445BG Historian.

APPENDIX

A U.S. 8TH AIR FORCE HEAVY BOMBER COMBAT BOX FORMATION IN WWII

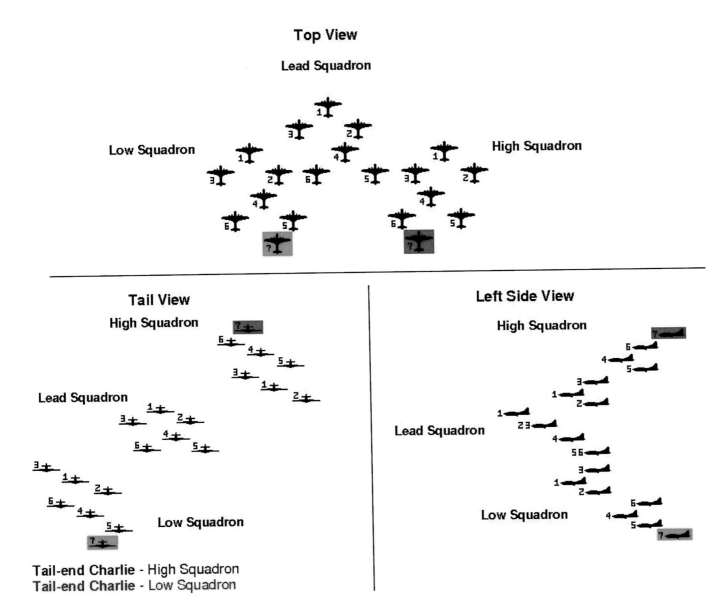

Illustration courtesy of the 303rd Bomb Group Association at http://www.303rdbg.com/formation.jpg and Gary L. Moncur. This type of formation was used by both four-engine heavy bombers, B-17s (below) and B-24s. Photos below are of the Collings Foundation B-17 *Nine O Nine* at Monmouth Executive Airport in NJ. Author's photos.

Below (l to r): Other WWII bombers for comparison - A B-29 Superfortress (Very Heavy), which is the type that dropped the atomic bombs on Japan; and the medium-sized B-25 Mitchell and B-26 Marauder. Author's collection.

The author, wearing a replica WWII U.S. Army Air Force A-2 bomber jacket and enlisted man's uniform, at the 445th Bomb Group's memorial marker at Tibenham Airfield, England on June 30, 2012. The words on the marker are printed below. Photo courtesy of Tony Griffiths. The memorial was dedicated on May 25, 1987, during a 2nd Air Division reunion.

445TH BOMBARDMENT GROUP (H)
2ND COMBAT WING 2ND AIR DIVISION
8TH UNITED STATES AIR FORCE
4TH NOVEMBER 1943 TO 28TH MAY 1945
FROM THIS AIRFIELD THE 445TH BOMBARDMENT GROUP LAUNCHED
280 MISSIONS AND FLEW 6323 SORTIES
THIS MEMORIAL IS HUMBLY DEDICATED TO THE 445TH BOMB GROUP
IN MEMORY OF THOSE AIRMEN WHO GAVE THEIR LIVES
AND THOSE WHO SERVED FIGHTING
FOR THE LIBERATION OF EUROPE DURING WORLD WAR II

700TH BS. 701ST BS.   702ND BS. 703RD BS.

Photo taken on October 7, 1943,
at Sioux City Army Air Base, Iowa
just before going overseas.
The new nose turret was washed out of
the photo because it was top secret.

445TH BOMBARDMENT GROUP (HEAVY)
703RD BOMB SQUADRON

THE WILLIAMS B-24 LIBERATOR CREW

Aircrew positions and ranks as of February 25, 1944

Top Row from L to R:

1st Lt. William "Mack" Williams - Pilot
2nd Lt. Douglas Pillow - Co-pilot
2nd Lt. Jesse Cummings - Navigator
2nd Lt. John "Jack" Heany - Bombardier
T/Sgt. George Snook - Flight Engineer/Top Turret Gunner

Bottom Row from L to R

S/Sgt. Joe Minton - Tail Gunner and Armorer
S/Sgt. Billy Fields - Right Waist Gunner and Armorer
T/Sgt. Frank Mangan - Radio Operator
M/Sgt. Grant Murray - Ground Crew Chief/Non-Flying
S/Sgt. Henry "Hank" Culver - Ball Turret Gunner, Left Waist Gunner
and Assistant Engineer
S/Sgt. Henry Going - Left Waist Gunner

The Williams crew flew *Nine Yanks and a Jerk* on a mission to bomb Nurnberg, Germany on February 25, 1944. Below they're seen in front of their original plane, *"Hap" Hazard*.

Oct. 7 – 43
Sioux City
Iowa.

445TH BOMBARDMENT GROUP (HEAVY), 703RD BOMB SQUADRON
THE B-24 CREW OF "HAP HAZARD" ★ THE WILLIAMS' CREW
TOP ROW (LEFT TO RIGHT): 2ND LT. WILLIAM "MACK" WILLIAMS (PILOT), 2ND LT. DOUGLAS PILLOW (COPILOT),
2ND LT. JESSE CUMMINGS (NAVIGATOR), 2ND LT. JACK HEANY (BOMBARDIER), TECH/SGT. GEORGE SNOOK (ENGINEER)
BOTTOM ROW (LEFT TO RIGHT): S/SGT. JOE MINTON (TAIL GUNNER), S/SGT. BILLY FIELDS (RIGHT WAIST GUNNER), TECH/SGT.
FRANK MANGAN (RADIO OPERATOR), MASTER/SGT. GRANT MURRAY (GROUND CREW CHIEF/NON-FLYING),
S/SGT. HENRY "HANK" CULVER (BALL TURRET & WAIST GUNNER), S/SGT. HENRY GOING (LEFT WAIST GUNNER)

1943   1945
445TH COMBAT GROUP H
2ND COMBAT WING
2ND AIR DIVISION
TIBENHAM
ENGLAND
8TH AIR FORCE
DEDICATED MAY

The 445th Bomb Group memorial at the U.S. Air Force Museum in Dayton, Ohio. Both photos taken on April 17, 2012

70TH ANNIVERSARY VISIT TO TIBENHAM AIRFIELD

Below is a photo taken of our tour group at the end of the runway at Tibenham Airfield where *Nine Yanks and a Jerk* skidded off into the field. Tony Griffiths was kind enough to get us clearance to drive to the end of the active runway and have time to reflect and take the photo.

Our WWII 70th Anniversary tour group – *The Daylight Raiders Tour* (l to r): Marlo (Williams) Hillstrom and her husband Doug, Mike Womack, Claire and Christine Muhlbauer, my mother Joan Culver, Chris Pillow, Tony Griffiths, and me. It was a very moving and memorable day for us all as we reflected upon the events of 70 years ago.

The author holding a framed print of **"Daylight Raiders,"** which portrays *Nine Yanks and a Jerk* at the moment of impact by a German .88mm shell that did not explode on the mission to bomb Nurnberg, Germany on February 25, 1944.

PRINT ORDERING

The *Daylight Raiders* print is available at www.Amazon.com.
The painting was made by aviation artist Jason Breidenbach in 2011.
The print includes a detailed description of the mission and what the scene portrays.
Quotes from several crew members are included, as well as the names, ranks, and positions of each
crew member at the time of the mission. The 703rd Bomb Squadron patch is also displayed on the print.
The aircrews' medals received by most of the crew are included as well.

The *Daylight Raiders* print

AIRCREW MEDALS DESCRIPTIONS

THE DISTINGUISHED FLYING CROSS AND THE AIR MEDAL

The DFC was awarded to those who completed their required 30 missions tour of duty,
for extraordinary achievement, and great courage and skill shown while in aerial combat.
The Air Medal was awarded to each crew member several times for participation in aerial combat over
Europe for every five to seven missions completed and for exceptionally meritorious service.

ACKNOWLEDGEMENTS

The compilation of this book is the result of research for a larger work about my father's combat experiences with his aircrew in World War II, called *Daylight Raiders*. As with the writing of the larger work, this book is the result of over four and a half years of intense research, extensive travel, and numerous personal interviews, not to mention a lifetime of hearing my father tell his stories which I never grew tired of listening to. It is also is a significantly expanded and updated version of an earlier unpublished draft of this work. The years of research, travel, and interviews have added immensely to this collection. I had sent all of the surviving families a comprehensive questionnaire to fill out about their loved ones' WWII service and overall lifetime history. The majority of them thoughtfully took the time to fill it out and send me the information. The responses have been wonderful.

Below is a substantial section acknowledging the many people involved with this work. A more detailed acknowledgment section is contained in the larger work, *Daylight Raiders*. The individual acknowledgements below are directly related to this book and are expanded in the larger book. The numerous people I have met over the last four and a half years have been incredible. It makes me realize all the more the old adage, "No man is an island." That truth has be borne out in this volume.

I am always so grateful to my family for being incredibly loving, supportive and encouraging in this work. My mother Joan (who proofread), my sister Debbie, and my brother Bill and his wife Janice have all been so excited and helpful from the start to see my father and his crew honored this way. They have shared what they have heard from my father, and whatever photos or records they knew about concerning his entire life and WWII service.*

My nephew Jason and his wife Christine, and their three children Kirsten, Samantha, and Justin are also excited and very on board with this project, and they have learned much about their grandfather and

The Culver family - Father's Day, June 17, 2008. From l to r: Hank Jr., Debbie, me, Janice, Bill, Joan and Hank Culver, Sr. My father was three months shy of his 85th birthday here. His recall of his WWII experiences was still sharp even after 64 years since those events. Photo courtesy of Bill and Janice Culver.

* My oldest brother Hank Jr., unexpectedly passed away in August of 2011, just six and half months after my father. The year 2011 was a tough year, first with the passing away of my father in February, followed by my Uncle Al Carreno, his mother Josephine Carreno, and then my brother – all on my father's side of the family.

great-grandfather and his service in WWII. They also proudly display the print of *Daylight Raiders* in their home.

My brother Bill, Jason, and I (pictured below) flew on a B-24 in September of 2011 to honor my father, and to experience a taste of what he knew very well in training and combat. My family has accompanied me at various times, and have shared in in many ways, much of what I've learned about my father and his crew. This has largely happened through what's been collected and gathered via the photos and research discovered throughout these last four and a half years. They have all been participants and benefactors in my journey of discovery. There's nothing like family, and this is one of the most important parts of my father's legacy. If he had not survived the war, none of us would be here.

September 4, 2011. About seven months after my father passed away, me, my brother Bill, and our nephew Jason flew on the Collings Foundation B-24J Liberator *Witchcraft* at Monmouth Executive Airport in Wall Township, New Jersey. We took the flight to honor our Dad and Jason's grandfather. It was a great tribute to his memory and his World War II service in the U.S. Army Air Forces. It was a thrill for all three of us to experience such a flight. We experienced a little taste of what my father knew very well, as he had hundreds of flying hours in this type of aircraft, both in training and in combat. This is the only flying B-24J model in the world. It is the same type and model my father and his crew flew in during the war. I was wearing a replica U.S. Army Air Force summer uniform like my father had worn during the war. Bill and Jason were wearing current U.S. Army ACUs. Bill retired in November of 2010 after 42 years of active and reserve military service – 14 years in the Navy and 28 years in the Army. Jason is a veteran police officer in central New Jersey.

My father's dear sister, Gloria Muhlbauer, my aunt, has been thrilled about this project, and the larger one, from the beginning. My aunt has been so kind to allow me to interview her for several hours

My father's sister, my Aunt Gloria (at age 90), with my mother Joan and my sister Debbie and me on Christmas Day 2012

at various times. Either at family gatherings or over the phone, she always was accommodating at every opportunity. Her memory has been incredibly sharp from ages 89 to 93. She and my father both served in WWII - she in the U.S. Coast Guard, while he was in the U.S Army Air Forces. Her three daughters, my cousins Claire, Christine, Marianne, and her son Paul and his wife Joan have also been so enthusiastic. Claire has allowed me access to her family's extensive photo collection also. Claire and Christine even accompanied me and my mother as we took some of the crew members' families to England with us in June of 2014 for a 70th anniversary tour to retrace my father's crew's footsteps and flight paths. We also honored their late father Louis's WWII U.S. Army service. Our tour group photo is included in this work. Claire and I often joked that she is my PR (Public Relations) person because of her enthusiasm, support, and PR experience.

Many family members on my mother's side of the family have been excited and encouraging as well. The following have seen some of the photos and photo books I have done as test prints. My Aunt Gloria Spohn is always thrilled to see my travel photos and hear the latest updates. Her daughter Linda and her husband John have also been encouraging and of assistance with legal questions related to this work and the larger one. My Uncle Jesse Freeman and his two daughters, my cousins Carol and her husband Dave along with Barbara and her husband Tom have also expressed their best wishes for my endeavors. Carol's son Kevin and Barbara's son Aaron have also shown interest in the success of this

George and Barbara Snook and me at our favorite restaurant near Springfield, Ohio. April 13, 2014

work. Everyone has said that it is a great way to honor my father, his crew, and their bomb group.

I am especially indebted to, and eternally grateful for, the crew's last surviving member – their flight engineer and top turret gunner Tech. Sergeant George Snook. George has so patiently allowed me to interview him in person on five separate trips at his home in Ohio, as well as at the U.S. Air Force Museum in Dayton, and also at the Champaign Air Museum at Grimes Field in Urbana, Ohio. We have also spoken on the phone dozens of times in the last four years since my father passed away in February of 2011. Keep in mind, George was between the ages of 90 to 94 as I interviewed him. George's keen recollection and great anecdotes are the things movies are made of. He and his wife Barbara have been so gracious to me, along with their children Thomas and Melody. I even stayed over George and Barbara's home as a guest. All have been a tremendous part of this project. They are like family to me. Because of George's meticulous checks on the readiness of the planes they flew, and his skills as their top turret gunner, without a doubt the entire crew was indebted to him, as well as their descendants. Their aircrew worked very well together, where each man played his part, yet all would agree that George was a key player. I often refer to George as a 'Top Gun' not only because he was the crew's top turret gunner, but because he is also a top notch guy. This work would not be as complete without George's accurate, detailed recollections and enthusiasm. In a big way, because of his thoroughness as a flight engineer and top turret gunner, he and the crew survived their tour of duty, and I'm also here to write this work (which he and I often reflect upon with a grateful chuckle). We're all indebted to you George. I thank you and Barbara also for proof reading this manuscript as well.

The surviving crew members' families have also been of tremendous help, encouragement, and endless support. They have sent photos, allowed me to look at their father's military files and records, and have answered numerous questions via phone, e-mail, and in person. Some have even had me stay at their homes as a guest, and were very gracious hosts. In addition, many have become good friends to me as well. The family of the crew's right waist gunner and armorer, Billy Fields, have been very obliging. Jane (Fields) Deeds and her husband Chuck, along with their son Dan and his family, all in Florida, have assisted me in my research at every request. Jane and Chuck invited me to stay at their home (formerly Billy and his wife's Charlene's home) in the spring of 2013. We had a wonderful time together.

On April 8, 2013, I posed for this candid shot with Billy Fields' daughter Jane (Fields) Deeds, her husband Chuck, their son Dan, and his two boys. Jane and I are holding her father's WWII U.S. Army Air Force dress uniform in front of her parents' home in Florida. It was her father, Billy, who saved my father's life on a mission to bomb Berlin, Germany on April 29, 1944. Photo taken by Dan's wife Darcy.

It was Billy Fields who saved my father's life on a later mission (to be detailed in the larger work). Chuck also took me on a tour of their local area, and to Billy's gravesite, where I paid my respects to the man who saved my father's life.

The pilot, Mack Williams' daughter Marlo (Williams) Hillstrom and her husband Doug, in Colorado, both accompanied me on

Mack Williams' daughter, Marlo (Williams) Hillstrom, posed for these two shots with me and her husband Doug near their home in Colorado on November 10, 2012.

the trip to England mentioned above. They both have been very closely involved in this project. They also invited me to stay at their home, in Colorado, back in November of 2012. We spent two days

pouring over Mack's military files and photos, and had a great time together. Doug scanned and copied what seemed like endless amounts of photos and documents. Marlo and I went through boxes of her father's records and photos. They also gave me a nice tour around the area and also took me to a nearby air museum near Peterson Air Force Base. They've become like family as well. We also recently spent a week together in Tucson, Arizona, in April of 2015. Doug used his retired U.S. Air Force colonel status to get me a room on base at Davis-Monthan Air Force base. I stayed just down the road from their on-base trailer

Co-pilot Douglas Pillow's son Christopher and his oldest daughter Melissa Pillow Herron in front of the Collings Foundation B-24 Liberator **Witchcraft** in Fort Collins, Colorado in 2011. This was the same plane my brother Bill, my nephew Jason, and I flew in that same year. Photo courtesy Christopher Pillow.

park where they had their RV. We toured around the area attractions, including the Pima Air Museum and the U.S. Air Force 'Boneyard' at Davis-Monthan AFB. It was a great week! Thank you both again. Thank you also for proof reading this manuscript.

Douglas Pillow's sons, Christopher (in Colorado), Arthur (in Arkansas), and Stephen (in Florida), have also gone out of their way to help. We have spoken on the phone, shared e-mail responses, and sent files back and forth to one another. Christopher also accompanied me on the tour to England. We had a great time. We also share that unique tie as having retraced our fathers' footsteps together.

The radio operator, Frank Mangan, has a daughter, Christine (Mangan) Homa (in Texas), who has openly shared her father's WWII scrapbook, diaries, and photos with me via her cousin Ron Decker (in California). Ron tirelessly photographed everything mentioned at Christine's former home in upstate New York and gave me all of it on a memory stick. Ron has been to our home twice in 2011 and 2012 to share his uncle's experiences with me face to face. Like me, Ron also shares a love for family genealogical research. He was definitely the ideal connection with Frank's family. We actually connected via Ancestry.com. This work would not be as complete without Ron's help.

Ron Decker visited me and my mother at our home in New Jersey in October of 2011. Ron shared his memories of his uncle, Frank Mangan, with us.

153

The bombardier, Jack Heany's wife Dorothy (in New Hampshire), and their daughter Anne and her husband Charlie (in Maryland), have been a tremendous help in answering questions, phone calls, and e-mails. Dorothy and I met face to face in August of 2012. Jack and Dorothy's grandson Brendan

Me and Dorothy Heany at her home in New Hampshire. We spent several hours sharing photos and documents about Jack's and my father's WWII service together. August 2012.

was also at Dorothy's home when I interviewed her. The three of us shared our families' histories and got each other caught up on the last 60 years since Jack and Dorothy lost contact with my father. I'm also so indebted to Anne for all that she did, with the help of her mother, during the years 2011 through early 2013. The details of my research wouldn't be nearly as complete otherwise. Anne provided me with the extensive details of her father's WWII experiences with photos and personal letters from him to her mother. Sadly, Anne passed away from a brain tumor in September of 2013 after months of treatments. The passing of Anne was and is a tremendous loss and sorrow. It was quite a shock. Before her passing, Anne gave me her brother, Jack Jr.'s phone number. Jack Jr. (in California) and I have since spoken on the phone also. Jack gave me some insight into some of his father's experiences during the war, and has offered to help in my research. My father was Jack Sr.'s best man at his and Dorothy's wedding back in the States in September of 1944.

The navigator, Jesse Cummings' daughter, Penny (Cummings) Cluff (in California), has sent me CD versions of an interview she recorded with her father just weeks before he passed away. She has also answered numerous e-mails, and a phone call, over the years. Her sister Patti (Cummings) Bean has also been supportive and enthusiastic about the work. They are also looking forward to the larger work as well.

Tail gunner Joe Minton's family (from l to r) his son William Eugene "Gene," grandson Matthew and his wife Monica, James, and me at a local restaurant in Denham Springs, Louisiana. It was my first taste of Cajun food. We had a good time reminiscing about our fathers' service together in WWII. Photo taken on April 14, 2014.

The tail gunner, Joe Minton, has two sons – James and William Eugene "Gene." Both have been encouraging in this project. James has sent me numerous photos and military records from their father's collection. I met both men, and a few of their family members, at Joe's grave site in Louisiana in April of 2014. We later went out to dinner together, where I had my first taste of Cajun food. We had a very nice time. James has also written a short biography of his father's life which he forwarded to me.

The nose turret gunner and sometimes waist gunner and armorer, Henry Going, had only one relative I was able to track down – his cousin George Moore (in South

Carolina). George recalled some of Henry's personal stories and shared them with me via e-mails and a few phone calls. Henry is still one of the least known crew members. I'm hoping to connect with someone who might know more about him.

Special thanks go out to the Shiffer family who own and operate the Champaign Aviation Museum at Grimes Field Airport in Urbana, Ohio. Leah, and hers sons Dave and Eric, have shown me a very warm welcome. They also allow George to tell the story of *Nine Yanks and a Jerk* each week to visitors to the museum. I'm thankful to them and the staff and all of the volunteers who work tirelessly to keep the memories of our WWII veterans alive by developing their flying museum and static displays for everyone to enjoy and learn from. Randy Kemp, who oversees the restoration of the B-17 *Champaign Lady* at the air museum, has been a great help by explaining many aviation facts and the workings of a heavy bomber to me, showing me around, and allowing me access to their facilities. Their website is filled with great photos and loads of information about WWII and what they're about. See http://www.champaignaviationmuseum.org.

George Snook and the author at the Champaign Aviation Museum at Grimes Field Airport in Urbana, Ohio on November 8, 2014. I interviewed George at age 93 on location at the hangar where he volunteers to help in the restoration of the B-17 Flying Fortress behind us. George gives talks to visitors about the history of his and my father's crew and bomb group. He also tells the story of their mission on February 25, 1944 to bomb Nurnberg, Germany in the B-24 Liberator *Nine Yanks and a Jerk*. The painting, *Daylight Raiders*, is also a framed poster print, which is just behind us and to my right. Photos of George and my father and their crew are on George's left. This was my fourth visit out to Ohio to see George and interview him. George is always accommodating and up for sharing his WWII experiences.

155

Above: George Snook's replacement A-2 bomber jacket with *Nine Yanks and a Jerk* painted on it by artist Frank Drain. The 30 bombs represent his 30 combat missions. The image is based on the painting and print done by aviation artist Jason Breidenbach for this book cover and for *Daylight Raiders*. Photos from Carole Buchwalter, December 2012. Below: George Snook at age 94 in front of the Collings Foundation B-24 *Witchcraft* in Ohio. George told the story of *Nine Yanks and a Jerk* in front of the plane. The print *Daylight Raiders* and the bomber jacket are on the easel next to him. George flew on this B-24 the day of this photo – August 15, 2015. It was his first flight in a B-24 since WWII - 70 years ago. Photo courtesy of Greg Schafer.

George Snook and Randy Kemp with the Champaign Air Museum's Flying Laboratory Experimental plane behind them. Photo taken on April 20, 2011, on my first trip, when I drove out to Ohio to meet George and Randy and get the tour of the museum. It was a wonderful trip.

Randy has allowed me multiple opportunities to interview George Snook at the site where he volunteers. The crew there has also allowed me to participate in some of their events as a guest and have welcomed me like a long-time friend. Their hospitality has been first rate.

Special thanks also go out to Red Ketchum, George's volunteer buddy and fellow WWII airmen. Red flew in B-17s as a ball turret gunner in the war. Red has also been so patient and kind to video and photograph me and George numerous times, both at the air museum in Urbana and at the U.S. Air Force Museum in Dayton. Norm Burmaster and Greg Schafer have also photographed and filmed us on numerous occasions. They have also sent me many e-mails with photos and updates on George and his activities. Bob and Carole Buchwalter have also sent me photos of George and his A-2 bomber jacket painted with the image of *Nine Yanks and a Jerk* on it. Thanks also to Jack Bailey and Greg for setting up George's display stands for his WWII talks at the Champaign Aviation Museum, and who have assisted me as well on some of my visits and projects. Many folks have been blessed to hear George retell his and my father's crew's stories, especially the one contained within this work, with the visual aids on display there.

I have made several trips out to the National Museum of the U.S. Air Force in Dayton, Ohio for many photo ops and research treks. The staff there has always been very accommodating to me with my camera and video equipment. I have taken hundreds of photos there over the years and shot many hours of video. Mona Vollmer, Colonel (USAF Retired), their Chief Development Officer, has allowed George, Red, and me extensive access to the displays for filming, photography and interviewing. Other staff members and volunteers have assisted me in many ways over the years as well. It is always a pleasure visiting the museum. I never grow tired of it. To me it is also a history of my family's involvement and participation in the U.S. military.

Norm Burmaster and me at a Veterans Day event at the museum on November 8, 2014. Norm periodically sends me photos and updates about George's volunteer work, talks, and guest appearances.

I'm also grateful to the family of Colonel Paul Schwartz. I initially contacted his daughter Carol and her husband Charles Funk at their home in Tampa, Florida through a written letter with photos included of Colonel Schwartz decorating my father and George Snook with the Distinguished Flying Cross, and one of him in front of the B-24 *Majorie*, named after his wife. After confirming that I had the correct family, Paul's grandson, Brian Funk, called me at the phone number I had forwarded. When he heard about the book I'm writing, Brian was kind enough to extend an invitation to his mother's home during a quick trip I was making through Florida in April of 2014. Since my time in town was short,

On November 8, 2014, the Champaign Aviation Museum had a Veterans Day Dinner and Dance night. Here Red Ketchum and I pose in front of his photo display. Red was a ball turret gunner on B-17s during the war. Red has photographed and shot video of George and me for many hours during our interviews.

they invited me for dinner one evening. They had a wonderful dinner prepared with all the trimmings in their beautiful home.

They shared Colonel Schwartz's life with me from his time growing up in Tampa, through the war, and his post-war life. We spent the better part of the late afternoon and early evening discussing Colonel Schwartz's WWII experiences along with me sharing photos of him decorating my father and George Snook at Tibenham Airfield in England. I also shared many photos of my father's WWII experiences. I answered some of their questions and helped them understand both men's WWII service together with the 445th Bomb Group.

In return for my gratitude for their hospitality and taking the time to meet with me, and in commemoration of our father's WWII service together, I gave them a framed photo of Colonel Schwartz decorating my father with the Distinguished Flying Cross, side-by-side with me in my father's WWII uniform standing next to the 445th Bomb Group Memorial at Tibenham Airfield from my 2012 trip. We had a great time together. It has proven to be a continued journey of discovery for both families as time goes by.

A special thanks to T/Sgt. Harold Eckelberry and his wife Janet of Tifflin, Ohio. Harold served in the same 703rd Bomb Squadron with my father in WWII. Jimmy Stewart had also flown with his crew. A photo of one of their missions with him is included in this work. Harold and Janet were kind enough to give me permission to include that photo

of Harold, his crew, and James Stewart. Janet was so kind to mail me copies of Harold's diary entries and mission descriptions from his WWII service. Harold likewise was thoughtful enough to sign an enlarged copy of the photo with James Stewart and Harold's crew.

The family of Walter Scott Buist, who also live in New Jersey, helped me with providing photos of their father and the plane *Nine Yanks and a Jerk*, which he too flew in as a replacement gunner with the original crew. Jim and Kevin Buist, Walter's sons, were very helpful in answering questions on the phone and through e-mails.

The Paul Schwartz family, from l to r: Harrison Tropp, Charles and Carol (daughter of Paul Schwartz) and their son Brian Funk, and me at Charles and Carol's home in Tampa, Florida. We had a great time talking about our father's WWII service together, and enjoyed a wonderful dinner in their home. Carol is holding the framed photo I had made for them. Photo taken on April 16, 2014.

They also provided me with some autobiographical material that their father wrote about his WWII experiences. The fact that their father flew on both the Ploesti and Kassel missions and lived to tell about them is astounding. It's a one in a million shot. He is the only man in the U.S. Army Air Force (whom I know of) who survived both disastrous missions, which were over a year apart and at different ends of the European Continent.

Walter Scott Buist with his grandson Walter Scott. Buist III, and sons Jim and Kevin in 2004 at the National WWII memorial in Washington D. C. Photo courtesy of Kevin Buist.

The National WWII Museum in New Orleans, Louisiana has also been accommodating in my research. I was able to take good photos there to illustrate my narrative. For example, the display of the German .88mm anti-aircraft gun (p.89) has helped to demonstrate the type of weapons the Germans used against our heavy bombers. Both sides of the war need to be told in order to appreciate what our men and women went through to achieve victory. The displays of aircraft, as well as land vehicles and landing craft are excellent. I look forward to another visit, as they have expanded since my initial visit in April of 2014.

The Pima Air Museum in Tucson, Arizona has been a great source for my research and photography. Their B-24 Liberator, **Bungay Buckaroo** (formerly **Shoot You're Covered**) is included in this work. The time and devotion by the staff and volunteers at such a museum helps to keep our aviation history alive and make it very tangible. The museum has been added to and expanded wonderfully since my father and I first visited it in May of 1988. It's nice to see how well-kept the B-24 and the many other planes are. The desert climate is truly ideal for the preservation of the aircraft there, not to mention it makes for a nice sunny day's visit. It provides a great educational experience.

The author in front of the National WWII Museum in New Orleans, Louisiana. The museum has several buildings which display different segments of WWII history. The building behind me is the US Freedom Center: The Boeing Pavilion, which houses some of the bomber and fighter planes used in the war. Other buildings house everything from tanks and cannons to D-Day landing craft, like the Higgins boat, which was built in New Orleans. There are also several theaters and video screens showing footage from WWII along with recent documentaries. Photo taken on April 15, 2015.

Me, Marlo (Williams) and her husband Doug Hillstrom at the Pima Air Museum in Tucson, Arizona in April 2015. I was able to visit this museum quite easily because Doug and Marlo were able to get me a very nice room at the nearby Air Force Inn on Davis-Monthan Air Force base in Tucson. Marlo and Doug winter there with their RV, and so Doug was able to used his retired Air Force colonel status to help me reserve a nice room on base. The Hillstroms have been so supportive of this project. We spent a week together in the Tucson area and had a great time. Doug and Marlo have both proofread this book several times for me.

Gear Up! In front of the B-24 Liberator *Bungay Buckaroo* at the Pima Air Museum. April 2015.

Many thanks are due to my British friends 'across the pond.' My good friends at the Norfolk Glider Club, which is based at Tibenham Airfield, have been so open to having me and the tour group as visitors. They also freely provided us space at their clubhouse and grounds for our re-enactment ceremony in June of 2014. Tony Griffiths, who is a member of the Norfolk Gliding Club, has taken me around the airfield at Tibenham numerous times each summer from 2012 through 2014. Tony has also flown me in their glider tow plane for a flight around the area in 2012. Tony led the tour group on a tour with access to their main runway to take photos at the

Tony Griffiths, Mike Bean, and Mike's grandson Adam (center) posed in front of the Norfolk Glider Club's tow plane. We took this shot right after Tony had taken me up for about a 40 minute flight in the plane to show me the area. We took off and landed on the same runway *Nine Yanks and a Jerk* did 68 years earlier at Tibenham. Photo taken on June 30, 2012.

end of the runway where *Nine Yanks and a Jerk* made its emergency landing in 1944. Back in 2012, Tony drove me around Norfolk County from Tibenham to Ketteringham Hall (where the 2nd Combat Wing Headquarters was) and around Hethel airfield (where the 389th Bomb group was based, which was a sister group to the 445th). He has also provided me with numerous photos of the airfield and

Mike Womack and me at the 445th Bomb Group memorial on July 8, 2012. It was Tibenham's first airshow that day. Unfortunately it was a rainy day, but as the weather broke a few planes did fly that day. Mike has been a great help in my research. Photo courtesy of Mike Womack.

Nissen hut areas over the years. Tony also led me on a walking tour of the airfield in 2012 and has a great working knowledge of the airfield and its history. He also took me to Seething Airfield, another nearby B-24 base, and got me special permission to tour the restored control tower and museum there (thanks to their staff). I wouldn't know the half of it without him. There's nothing like going to a location and having the locals explain things to you!

Special thanks to Berkeley Pittaway, who has driven me around the airfield at Tibenham several times, especially to where *Nine Yanks and a Jerk* skidded off the runway. He has shown me continual hospitality at their clubhouse. Berkeley even gave me a piece of the Tibenham runway in the summer of 2014 to take back home as a token of my father's WWII service and of my travels.

Mike Bean has been very helpful in connecting me with Tony and the rest of the staff when I first came over in 2012. I'm also thankful to Eddie and Rachel Applegate and April Banyard for allowing me to look through the Glider Club's library of photos. All of the staff and members at the Glider Club have been extremely helpful and have made me feel very welcome. Eddie and Rachel have also fed me many times, as well as the tour group, at the clubhouse.

Eric Ratcliffe is also to be thanked. In 2012, Eric gave me an extensive tour around the entire airfield and surrounding former Nissen hut sites, work areas, and to the local village and church. He also took me over to Hardwick airfield, another WWII B-24 air base about 10 miles away by car. There I was given a tour by the local farmer and owner of the property, an 86 year old gentleman named David. David took me to look inside some the original and restored Nissen huts and main buildings still standing at the site. This gave me a good idea of what once stood at Tibenham. While there I also got to see the fantastic WWII plane collection of Maurice Hammond of Hardwick Warbirds. I also saw their museum in the hangar. Eric then took me back to Tibenham. Eric was also the organizer of the July 2012 airshow at Tibenham, which I also attended. Eric has since helped me with photos of 445th Bomb Group planes and connected me with some veterans' families.

Rob Smith and Fawnda Mathison posed with me at The Greyhound Public House in Tibenham village on July 1, 2012. They both manage the pub. Suzie took me here to meet them and some other locals right after she met me.

Mike Womack, who lives just a few miles away from Tibenham, and I have also become good friends since I've made my first trip over in 2012. We met at the airshow there in July of 2012. We've continued to correspond via the internet. Mike even helped me get a vintage 1940s bicycle from England via Ebay.uk, and then

Suzie Vincent and I posed for this photo op on June 29, 2014. Suzie had missed us earlier at the 1940s event and ceremony and later drove into Norwich to meet up with me and the tour group that evening. She is a great friend and encouragement to me in this project. We retold our comical first meeting to everyone. Photos on this page courtesy of Suzie Vincent, and Marlo Hillstrom.

took photos and video of me riding it in a WWII uniform in the summer of 2013 near my father's former Nissen hut site and around Tibenham Airfield. Mike then helped me get the vintage bike shipped to the U.S. to my home in New Jersey. When I brought the tour group over in 2014, Mike had arranged for us to go to Ketteringham Hall for a photo shoot, and then to Thorpe Abbots (a former B-17 airfield) restored control tower and hut site for lunch and a wonderful tour. Mike also took numerous photos for us and handled the distribution of the posters I sent over of *Nine Yanks and a Jerk* and the aircrew photos. Thanks Mike!

Suzie and Hannah Vincent, who also live near the airfield, have been wonderful friends who have looked after me ever since Suzie drove past me and stopped as I was seen walking around the edge of the airfield in my father's WWII uniform and bomber jacket taking photos in the summer of 2012. Suzie's initial inquisitiveness about my doings led to a comical first meeting where she asked if I was late for the previous night's event. She thought that I had missed the previous night's WWII party at the local Greyhound Pub in the village of Tibenham. When I explained that I knew nothing about it, but was just over to visit my father's former air base and local village, she then drove me down the road to the village pub and introduced me to the owners, Rob and Fawnda, and a few other locals. As a result of her adventurous spirit, we now have a fun memory to talk about each time we tell the story. Our friendship and subsequent travels to Duxford Airfield airshow the following summer in 2013 with her, her daughter Hannah, and Hannah's boyfriend Tom, was another fun event and good memories. We also attended the Greyhound Pub's 1940s event later that evening in the village of Tibenham, that same day as the airshow. I was their guest of honor. At the 2014 WWII re-enactment and ceremony, Suzie and Hannah missed us initially due to a heavy downpour which soaked us all and flooded her property. Later that evening, Suzie searched for me and the tour group once we had left to go back to our hotel. She finally tracked us down at our Holiday Inn hotel in Norwich late that evening as we were finishing our dinner. She came dressed in a woman's WWII Royal Air Force uniform. We were so surprised and impressed by her diligence in seeking us out. I was still in my father's WWII uniform, so we took a few photos. She and Hannah came back to the hotel very early in the morning a couple of days later to see us off. She and Hannah then led me to the airport at Norwich where I

Hannah Vincent and her fiancee Tom at the Greyhound Pub in Tibenham at the 1940's event in July of 2013. Photo courtesy of Suzie Vincent.

dropped off my rental car. They both drove me back to the train station in Norwich and saw me off as I went to catch my train to Edinburgh, Scotland. They have proven to be more wonderful examples of British hospitality and friendship. Suzie also helped arrange the photo flight I took from Seething Airfield to Tibenham Airfield with her friend Brian Barr, a pilot based at Seething in July of 2015.

Mark Bancroft and the WWII re-enactors who so enthusiastically helped me re-enact in June of 2014 the 70th anniversary of my father's WWII award of the Distinguished Flying Cross ceremony are

to be commended for their dedication, enthusiasm, and authenticity. Mark helped

Mark Bancroft, me, Dave Tuthill, and a few British re-enactors dressed as American airmen from WWII at the 445th Bomb Group's memorial at Tibenham Airfield. Photo taken on July 8, 2012, the day of the airshow. The memorial wreath was laid down the week before by them in honor of the American airmen who served from this base in WWII.

coordinate the ceremony and made arrangements at Tibenham Airfield for our event. The tour group thoroughly enjoyed the jeep ride from the Greyhound Pub's green to the airfield at Tibenham for the ceremony. The entire ceremony was very moving for all who attended. It was one we'll never forget. Mark and his wife Sue and all of the re-enactors have been so encouraging and inspiring for this work and the larger one as well. They have offered helpful suggestions and comments.

Edouard Renière (in Belgium) and I connected via his internet website http://www.evasioncomete.org/ fschleisg.html. I was able to correspond with him and eventually got the story on the last crew who flew *Nine Yanks and a Jerk*. Because of this, I also came to realize that my father watched that crew get shot down on April 12, 1944. Through Edouard's webpage, and my additional research, I pieced together the story of the shoot down with my father's telling of it all my life. It was Edouard who then put me in touch with the Bombaerts, a family in Belgium who are very connected with the story of the downed pilot, Gilbert Shawn.

Rita and Freddy Bombaerts (in Belgium) were so kind to meet me at the crash site of *Nine Yanks and a Jerk* in Thorembais St. Trond near Perwez in July of 2014. After a few photos at the

Freddy and Rita Bombaerts, Josiane Flabat, me, and Christian Barbier at a local café near the crash site of *Nine Yanks and a Jerk* near Perwez, Belgium. I interviewed them for about two hours here. We had a few cups of tea and coffee, too. Photo July 8, 2014.

site, we then spent two hours in a local café with me interviewing them and their friends about the crash. It was Rita's father, Louis Mandelaire, who initially rescued the downed pilot, Gilbert Shawn, who was part of the last crew to fly the plane in April of 1944. They have been so kind and helpful.

Benjamin Heylen, a local museum curator, also met me at the site and took me on a tour of his museum and the local area. He showed me where Gilbert Shawn was hidden by the Belgian underground movement throughout the area. Benjamin also gave me a piece of the plane's wreckage as a token of my visit. He is also the one who connected me with Gilbert Shawn's son, Eric, the Fox News commentator here in the States. My research and the development of the story grew even more interesting.

A special thanks to Eric Shawn who has read this manuscript and added comments and suggestions. Eric has been a great encouragement and a welcomed surprise in this journey of discovery. My father witnessed his father's shoot down in *Nine Yanks and a Jerk* on its final mission on April 12, 1944. This was quite a surprise to both of us, as we both visited the crash site in the summer of 2014 (unknown to us, until I met Benjamin there), just weeks apart from each other. Eric and I grew up hearing about our own father's stories separately, but now understand and

Marcel Barras and Lauretta Verbist in front of Marcel's home in Thorembais St. Trond, Belgium. June 25, 2015.

appreciate them in greater detail.

Marcel Barras is the eyewitness I interviewed on my second trip to the crash site in June of 2015. I am amazed at how he was such a surprise discovery to this story. Marcel was so kind in letting us interview him outside his home on an unexpected visit from me and two new Belgian friends I made.

Lauretta Verbist was another wonderful surprise on the same day as Marcel. Without her help and willingness to take me over to the farm owner and to Marcel, I might not have had it so easy in making such a discovery. Because she acted as the translator between me and Marcel, I was able to get one of the incredible stories in this work. The farm owner was also key in leading us to Marcel and translating for me as well.

Brian Barr was patient and kind enough to fly me free of charge in his private plane and fly into Tibenham from Seething Airfield (another WWII B-24 base not too far from Tibenham) to get another view of Tibenham and other 8th Air Forces bases from the air. Suzie Vincent's friendship with Mike

helped to make this happen. Thanks to Brian, I was able to get additional video and still photos that will both add to this work and the larger one. He also opened up the Nissen hut museum at Seething Airfield for me to look at and take some photos. Brian also introduced me to Mike Page, another pilot based out of Seething Airfield. Mike Page has generously provided me with some of the photos of Tibenham for this work and *Daylight Raiders*. Mike also sent me links to several websites that proved to be very helpful.

Brian Barr standing on the wing of his plane at Seething Airfield on July 10, 2015. I flew in this plane with him for my aerial shots of Tibenham and other 8th Air Force bomber fields around Norfolk and Suffolk Counties, England.

Charlie Doggett, nephew of Earl Doggett, has allowed me to use photos from his tribute webpage about his uncle Earl Doggett who was part of the original crew of *Nine Yanks and a Jerk*. Earl and most of the original crew went missing in action over the North Sea on the 445th Bomb Group's mission to Syracourt, France on February 2, 1944, only on another plane. Charlie and I have corresponded and have compared notes about his uncle's and my father's experiences flying in the uniquely named plane. His tribute page can be viewed at http://www.charliedoggett.net/joomla/index.php/family-history/family-history-intro/earl-doggett-war-hero/44-our-family-world-war-ii-hero.

Many thanks to Eric Van Slander and the staff at the National Archives in College Park, Maryland. I've made at least seven trips down the I-95 corridor to that location to search the 445th Bomb Groups folders. I often made the three and a half hour drive to see my father's mission records and other folders at the archives over the last four years. I'm recognized by face there now. Eric has helped me save time, locate the many mission folders, and helped me narrow my search for the U.S Army Air Forces Strategic Bombing Survey folders for every mission that my father flew in. The fifth floor Photographs room has also assisted me in helping me narrow my research inquiries there as well. I have spent over 120 hours at the Archives, and it has yielded much fruit and many pleasant surprises.

I would be remiss if I did not mention my haircutter and project enthusiast, Heidi, at Cache Salon in Warren, New Jersey. Heidi has given me the WWII military haircuts for all of my trips and photo shoots over these last four years. She's always excited to hear about my trips and see the photos I've taken, which display her handiwork. I told her that when we get a movie made from the book she will be on the set as an official haircutter. Heidi always has a positive word and a great outlook on life. Thanks for all of your support and enthusiasm!

I'm also thankful for the patience and hard work of Ngan "Nancy" Nguyen, my tailor, at Park Avenue Cleaners in South Plainfield, New Jersey. Nancy has tailored and dry-cleaned my WWII outfits for these past four and a half years. I've been to her for dozens of alterations, patches to be sewn on, and uniforms to be dry-cleaned countless times. She always has a smile and works very hard at what she does. She's been excited to hear about my travels and what I've worn at the many locations I've traveled to. Her boss, Ed Bialick, has also assisted me with the cleaning of the various outfits and uniforms I've worn as well. I appreciate their friendly service.

Mike Simpson, the web host of the 445th Bomb Group's website http://www.445bg.org, has assisted me numerous times over the years. Mike has patiently answered many of my questions, checked me on various facts, and allowed me to use many of the photos and a chart contained in this work and in the book to come. Mike also put together a Mission History booklet of my father's 30 combat missions for a reasonable price based on his records obtained from the National Archives. Thanks for all of your help Mike.

Dan Stockton at B-24 Best Web http://b24bestweb.com has allowed me to use many of the photos posted on his site. The site has proven to be an indispensable source for B-24 photos from public and private collections. It is the 'Mother Lode' of sites for any WWII B-24 enthusiast or researcher.

Additional thanks go out to Bob Migliardi at Iliad Design who has so generously allowed me to reproduce his nose art designs for decals for modeling *Nine Yanks and a Jerk*. His drawings of the plane, which portray it at the time my father and his crew flew it, aided in the artwork for the painting I had commissioned that this book helps to explain. It is also a very nicely produced decal package for anyone who would like to make a model of *Nine Yanks and a Jerk* either in a 1/48 or 1/72 scale model. Decals can be purchased at http://www.hyperscale.com/2011/reviews/decals/iliad72007decalreviewrk_1.htm.

Gary L. Moncur, at the 303rd Bomb group's website was kind enough to allow me to use the website's diagram of an 8th Air Force Combat Box formation diagram to help illustrate what B-17 and B-24 bomb groups had to assemble into for maximum firepower protection against enemy fighter attacks. As the saying goes, "a picture is worth a thousand words."

The Collings Foundation, which owns and operates the B-24J Liberator *Witchcraft*, continues to provide, within the continental United States, the only flying B-24 of this model in the world. Each year over three million people get to see the plane on its Wings of Freedom Tour as it stops at 120 cities in the U.S. I have purchased several flights on this aircraft over the last five years. They have allowed me numerous photo ops both inside and outside the plane both in flight and when it has been parked. Several photos are included in this work. As their website says, it is " a symbol of American patriotism and [is] a learning tool for our future generations to learn more about World War II and aviation history." http://www.collingsfoundation.org/ aircrafts/consolidated-b-24-liberator/.

Many of my former co-workers and administrators at Grant Elementary School and the South Plainfield Board of Education in New Jersey have been excited about this work from the start. As I shared my father's and his crew's photos, stories, and tales of their combat missions, they have been keenly interested to hear them. Each year I would share my father's stories, along with my travels in retracing his footsteps, through numerous slideshows during the school year with my students. Some of my colleagues and administrators sat in my classes to see the slideshows and to see me dressed in replica and real WWII uniforms like my father would have worn. A few of my biggest supporters who have gone out of their way to help me in this work are Michelle Kirchofer, Joanne Haus, Judy Dias, and Ellen Decker-Lorys. These women have also viewed some of my photo test print books, and have always had encouraging things to say about what I've been presenting and working on. I thank you for your encouragement throughout those years. It meant a lot. The same can be said for many other colleagues and administrators.

Michelle and I worked together in my classroom for four out of the five years we taught together as Social Studies teachers. Michelle got to see me in action daily during those years and was always encouraging and excited to hear what my latest research and travel experiences were. She was eager to see my latest slideshows and hear me tell the stories that went with them. She has also helped me with some research with her uncle whom I interviewed, who also served in B-24s in WWII, and will be described in the larger work. She also bought me a book and DVD set about WWII over the years. Michelle has read my earlier version of this manuscript and provided helpful and encouraging comments.

Joanne Haus, and her husband Kenny, both read the earlier unpublished draft of this work and shared some inspiring comments. Joanne's father also served in WWII. Our parents used to bowl together in a mixed league back in the 1960s. Judy Dias, whose father also served in WWII, was very encouraging and helpful to me with my first trip to England. Her husband, Randy, brought back a train map of stations and destinations from one of his trips to England so that I could find the right station and train to get from London to Norwich, which is near my father's WWII air base at Tibenham. Both women have also viewed my slideshows connected with this research and have shared encouraging comments.

Ellen, whose father served in WWII as well, has also been excited and supportive about this work. She stopped in my classroom often to view the slideshows related to this work, and was always interested to hear about my next adventure. As principal, Ellen also made sure that I got class coverage for my class so that I was able to go to another elementary school in the district in order to be part of their large Veterans Day program to honor my father and all veterans with. Ellen also helped me get my brother Bill, a retired U.S. Navy and Army veteran of 42 years, to come into my classroom in uniform and present his military service for a Veterans Day lesson. It was a planned surprise for my niece Kirsten who was in my class that year.

David Zung, professor of Cinematography at NYU and fellow WWII enthusiast, has befriended me and has become a great advocate for the book and the pursuit of making it into a movie. David and I met at Morristown Airport in New Jersey in October of 2014. We were both shooting video and still photos of the Collings Foundation's B-24 Liberator *Witchcraft* when we struck up a conversation. I was dressed in a WWII summer flight suit with a Mae West life vest, canvas helmet, and goggles (like the one shown on the following page). After explaining to David what I was doing, we wound up conversing and shooting video for three and a half hours. He shot hours of professional footage of me and the B-24 that day. Since that day, David has offered to help me shoot a movie trailer in order to help promote the larger work and to eventually get it made into a movie. He continues to be a great encouragement and help in this project. We continue to shoot video and stills for the movie trailer as of this writing. Several of the scenes portray what's described in this book. He has been a great friend, producer, cinematographer, acting coach, and a great source of encouragement. Thanks for all that you're doing David! I'm also thankful to his wife Susan who is so patient in allowing him to spend time throughout the week and on some weekends to shoot the various scenes. As we talked through the scenes, it has also helped me to better narrate this work. This is a large part of his profession.

And finally, many thanks are due to my aviation artist and friend, Jason Breidenbach. I met Jason at the WWII Weekend at Reading Airport in Reading, Pennsylvania in June of 2011, just four months after my father passed away. It was my first time at this annual event. While walking through the display hangar, I saw Jason's fantastic artwork showcased and knew immediately that he was the one I wanted to commission to paint my father's famed WWII plane. Jason has done so well in accurately portraying the plane *Nine Yanks and a Jerk* on it mission to bomb Nurnberg, Germany on February 25, 1944, that many people have looked at the painting and thought that it was a photograph. Jason was very patient with my requests for certain details and accuracy based on the eyewitness accounts, U.S. Army Air Force records, and the photos taken of the plane in WWII. His artwork serves not only as part of the cover of this book, but also is the cover art for my webpage, *Daylight Raiders*.

A WORK OF ART

June 8, 2013. Me and Jason Breidenbach, the aviation artist who painted *Daylight Raiders* - the painting of *Nine Yanks and a Jerk* on its February 25, 1944 mission to bomb Nurnberg, Germany. The photo was taken at the Mid-Atlantic Air Museum's annual WWII Weekend at Reading Airport in Reading, Pennsylvania. I was wearing a summer flight suit, a real WWII Mae west life vest, canvas flight helmet, and replica goggles like my father wore. Jason rented a corner display in the Spaatz hangar at the airport. This is the same location where I met him two years earlier and had asked him to paint the scene that we're standing on either side of. Jason's artwork is so realistic that many have thought the painting to be a photograph. Jason has also produced a styrofoam cutout version of the plane with the same markings as shown in the print. Jason can be contacted via his website at http://www.jbaviationart.com.

BIBLIOGRAPHY

BOOKS

Astor, Gerald. *The Mighty Eighth: The Air War in Europe as Told by the Men Who Fought It*. New York: D.I. Fine, 1997. Print.

Birdsall, Steve. *B-24 Liberator in Action*. Warren, MI: Squadron/Signal Publications, 1975. Print.

Bowman, Martin W. *B-24 Combat Missions: First-hand Accounts of Liberator Operations over Nazi Europe*. New York: Fall River, 2009. Print.

Caldwell, Donald L. *JG 26 Luftwaffe Fighter Wing Diary: Volume Two: 1943-45*. Mechanicsburg, PA: Stackpole, 2012. Print.

Caldwell, Donald L. *JG 26: Photographic History of the Luftwaffe's Top Guns*. Osceola, WI: Motor International, 1994. Print.

Caldwell, Donald L. *JG 26 Top Guns of the Luftwaffe*. New York: Ivy, 1991. Print.

Craven, W.F. *Army Air Forces in World War II... Vol.2. - EUROPE: TORCH TO POINTBLANK AUGUST 1942 TO DECEMBER 1943*. University of Chicago, 1949. Print.

Freeman, Roger Anthony., Alan Crouchman, and Vic Maslen. *Mighty Eighth War Diary*. London: Jane's, 1981. Print.

Freeman, Roger Anthony. *Mighty Eighth War Manual*. London: Jane's, 1984. Print.

Hammel, Eric M. *Air War Europa: America's Air War against Germany in Europe and North Africa, 1942-1945: Chronology*. Pacifica, CA: Pacifica, 1994. Print.

Hammel, Eric M. *The Road to Big Week: The Struggle for Daylight Air Supremacy over Western Europe, July 1942-February 1944*. Pacifica, CA: Pacific Military History, 2009. Print.

Hoppes, Jonna Doolittle. *Calculated Risk: The Extraordinary Life of Jimmy Doolittle, Aviation Pioneer and World War II Hero; a Memoir*. Santa Monica, CA: Santa Monica, 2005. Print.

Infield, Glenn B. *Big Week: The Classic Story of the Crucial Air Battle of WWII*. Washington: Brassey's (US), 1993. Print.

Keeney, L. Douglas. *The Pointblank Directive: Three Generals and the Untold Story of the Daring Plan That Saved D-day*. Oxford: Osprey, 2012. Print.

Mackay, Ron, Mike Bailey, and Steven Adams. *Second in Line - Second to None: A Photographic History of the 2nd Air Division*. Atglen: Schiffer, 2014. Print.

Miller, Donald L. *Masters of the Air: America's Bomber Boys Who Fought the Air War against Nazi Germany*. New York: Simon & Schuster, 2006. Print.

Minton, Joe E. *Ten Men and a Bomber*. N.p.: Unpublished, 1992. Print.

Morrison, Wilbur H. *Fortress without a Roof: The Allied Bombing of the Third Reich*. New York, NY: St. Martin's, 1982. Print.

Robinson, John Harold. *A Reason to Live*. Memphis, TN: Castle, 1988. Print.

Smith, Starr. *Jimmy Stewart: Bomber Pilot*. St. Paul, MN: Zenith, 2005. Print.

Steinbeck, John. *Bombs Away!* New York, NY: Viking, 1942. Print.

Yenne, Bill. *Big Week: Six Days That Changed the Course of World War II*. New York: Berkley, 2013. Print.

Zaloga, Steve. *Operation Pointblank 1944: Defeating the Luftwaffe*. Long Island City, NY: Osprey, 2011. Print.

WEBPAGES

American Air Museum at Duxford. http://www.iwm.org.uk/visits/iwm-duxford.

Axis History. http://forum.axishistory.com/viewtopic.php?f=5&t=9174&p=7739.

B24 Best Web. http://b24bestweb.com.

B24.NET - 392nd. http://www.b24.net/ books/furth.htm.

B24.NET - WWII B-24 Liberator Bomber & WW2 POW Stalag Luft Camps of USAAF Army Air Force." *B24.NET - WWII B-24 Liberator Bomber & WW2 POW Stalag Luft Camps of USAAF Army Air Force*.

Breidenbach, Jason. http://www.jbaviationart.com.

Caldwell, Don. http://www.don-caldwell.we.bs/jg26/26kd2.htm.

Champaign Aviation Museum, Home of the B-17 Warbird Restoration. http://www.champaignaviationmuseum.org.

The Collings Foundation - Preserving Living Aviation History. http://www.collingsfoundation.org/ aircrafts/consolidated-b-24-liberator.

Doggett, Charlie. "Home." http://www.charliedoggett.net/joomla/index.php/family-history/family-history-intro/earl-doggett-war-hero/44-our-family-world-war-ii-hero.

Escape and Evasion. http://www.evasioncomete.org/fschleisg.html.

8th Air Force. http://www.mightyeighth.org/Library/PDFs/8thAFfacts.pdf

8th Air Force Fighter Group - Littlefriends.co.uk. http://www.littlefriends.co.uk/gallery.

8th Air Force Historical Society. http://www.8thafhs-pa.org/stories/bomb-group-gallery/44th-bomb-group.

FDR Library. Photo of Franklin D. Roosevelt, Winston Churchill, and Combined Chiefs of Staff at the Casablanca Conference in Casablanca, Morocco in January 1943. Courtesy of the Franklin D. Roosevelt Library and Museum at https://fdrlibrary.wordpress.com; version November 1, 2015

Fold3. - *Historical Military Records*. http://www.fold3.com.

Fox News. http://www.foxnews.com/ on/personalities/ericshawn/bio.

Global Aviation. http://www.globalaviationresource.com/v2/2014/02/20/d-day-70-pt-3-operation-argument-the-big-week-bomber-offensive-february-1944.

The Greyhound Public House. http://www.the-greyhound-tibenham.co.uk/.

Google Maps. https://www.google.com/maps.

Henri-Chapelle American Cemetery. https://www.abmc.gov/cemeteries-memorials/europe/henri-chapelle-american-cemetery#.VcJCVvlVhBc

Heylen, Benjamin. *Musee de Souvenir*. "http://www.museedusouvenir.be/.

History.com - American & World History. *HISTORY.com*.

Hobby Vista. http://fw190.hobbyvista.com/genth1.htm.

Hyperscale. http://www.hyperscale.com/2011/reviews/decals/iliad72007decalreviewrk_1.htm.

Imperial War Museums. http://www.iwm.org.uk/visits/iwm-duxford.

LeNox's Pastime. http://lenoxsthesaurus.blogspot.com/2010/01/thorembais-saint-trond.html.

Luftwaffe. http://www.luftwaffe.cz/radener.html.

Mighty Eighth Air Force Historical Society of WW2. *Mighty Eighth Air Force Historical Society of WW2*.

Migliardi, Bob. "ILIAD DESIGN." http://www.iliad-esign.com/decals/72morestars.html.

National Archives and Records Administration. http://www.archives.gov/.

National Museum of the US Air Force™. *National Museum of the USAF*.

National WWII Museum. http://nationalww2museum.org/.

Norfolk Gliding Club. http://www.norfolkglidingclub.com/.

Norfolk Historic Maps. http://www.historic-maps.norfolk.gov.uk.

Official Website of the 100th Bomb Group (Heavy) Foundation. http://www.100bgmus.org.uk/.

100% Female Brussels Airlines Crew Flies to New York on International Women's Day. http://press.brusselsairlines.com/100-female-brussels-airlines-crew-flies-to-new-york-on-international-womens-day.

Simpson, Mike. "445BG." www.445bg.org.

Terrill, Robert. http://www.af.mil/AboutUs/Biographies/Display/tabid/225/Article/105401/lieutenant-general-robert-h-terrill.aspx

398th Bomb Group Web Site. http://www.398th.org/.

303rd Bomb Group (H) - Molesworth, England. http://www.303rdbg.com/.

Tibenham Airfield (Norfolk Gliding Club)... (C) Evelyn Simak. *Geography of Britain and Ireland*. http://www.geograph.org.uk/photo/2230928.

Tibenham at War. *Tibenham at War*. http://www.tibenham.fsnet.co.uk/tib_at_war.htm.

UBI. http://forums.ubi.com/showthread.php/553263-B-24-Assembly-Ships-Released!-Forums.

Seething Control Tower Museum. http://www.seethingtower.org/.

Wikimedia Commons. https://commons.wikimedia.org/wiki/Main_Page.

Wikipedia. http://en.wikipedia.org/wiki/8.8_cm_Flak

WINGS PALETTE - News. http://wp.scn.ru/en/forum/in_focus/327-3-81

WWII in Color. CC-BY-SA-3.0-de], via Wikimedia Commons. http://www.ww2incolor.com/german-air-force/untitled_002.html

WW2 UK Airfields of the Eighth USAAF. http://www.controltowers.co.uk/8%20list%201.htm.

INDEX

ABOUT THE AUTHOR

Scott Culver's interest in World War II began with his father's telling of his wartime service and combat experiences to him as early as the age of five. His interest grew over the years as his father, Henry J. Culver, Sr., shared his experiences as a ball turret gunner, waist gunner, and assistant engineer on a B-24 Liberator crew in more detail. Scott developed a love for history, especially World War II history, as a result. Inspired by his father's patriotism and wartime service, Scott followed in his father's footsteps and enlisted in the United States Air Force after graduating from high school. After completing his Air Force Basic Training at Lackland Air Force Base in San Antonio, Texas, he served with the Military Airlift Command (MAC) division, where he served in ground support squadrons with the 438th Field Maintenance Squadron and in the 438th Transportation Squadron, both at McGuire Air Force Base in New Jersey. Scott also was able to fly on various missions during his service in the largest aircraft in the world at the time, the C-5 Galaxy transport plane. He also flew in the C-141 Starlifter transport repeatedly. While on active duty, he attended college in his off-duty hours and was able to accumulate college credits. After receiving an Honorable Discharge from his military service, Scott used his veteran's benefits and completed his college studies in the educational field, having earned two B.A. degrees with honors – one in Elementary Education, and another in Psychology. He later acquired a qualification in Middle School Social Studies. He has taught both American and World History courses, and Language Arts, in the elementary and middle school levels. He taught in private and public schools for over 20 years. Scott has spent the last four and a half years traveling the United States and Europe, several times each, retracing his father's WWII footsteps and flight paths. He interviewed his father's fellow crew members' families, as well as their last surviving combat crew member, George Snook. Many other individuals related to this work were interviewed as well. A considerable amount of those efforts are contained in this work. He continues to travel, research, and write for his larger work entitled, *Daylight Raiders,* and a photo essay called *Son of a Gunner*. The former volume encompasses his father's entire life, from growing up in New York City to his complete World War II training and 30 combat missions over Nazi occupied Europe from 1942 to 1944, and to the war's end as a gunnery instructor. Included will be a post-war section of his father's, his fellow crew members' and Jimmy Stewart's lives. Scott is also filming a movie trailer entitled *Daylight Raiders* as a promo for the book and to propel his father's life story into a major motion picture. He is an actor in the movie trailer portraying his father. The book *Son of a Gunner* is a photographic journal about his travels and research in writing the first two books. Scott wore his father's uniforms and flight gear to the places he trained and served at around the world, creating dozens of 'then and now' shots. In addition, Scott reenacts at WWII events as a bomber crewman in tribute to his father.

PHOTO COURTESY OF DOUG AND MARLO (WILLIAMS) HILLSTROM

Website: www.sonofagunnerb24.com Contact info: http://www.sonofagunnerb24.com/contact
or scott@sonofagunnerb24.com

COMING IN 2017

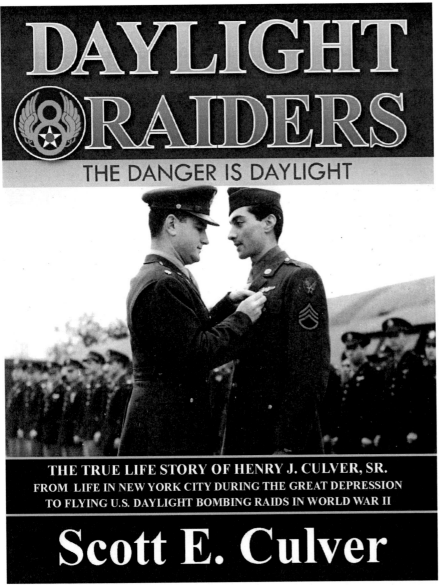

DAYLIGHT 8 RAIDERS

THE DANGER IS DAYLIGHT

THE TRUE LIFE STORY OF HENRY J. CULVER, SR.
FROM LIFE IN NEW YORK CITY DURING THE GREAT DEPRESSION
TO FLYING U.S. DAYLIGHT BOMBING RAIDS IN WORLD WAR II

Scott E. Culver

From tough city life in the 'concrete jungle' of New York to the deadly air space over Nazi occupied Europe, Hank Culver learned to fight for his life at an early age.

From the author

"It has been said, "Truth is stranger than fiction." This is something my father and I used to say to each other in relation to his life's story. The story of my father's life is something I had begged him to write since I was in grammar school. I grew up hearing him tell his almost unbelievable tales around the dinner table and at family gatherings about how he lived through the Great Depression and thirty combat missions in WWII. From tough city life in the 'concrete jungle' of New York to the deadly air space over Nazi occupied Europe, Hank Culver learned to fight for his life at an early age. I always said to him that he should write a book, and that it should be made into a movie. He would simply laugh and humbly agree. Although it wasn't his lot in life to be a writer, he sure could tell the stories well. After growing up hearing his stories for the forty-five years that I had him as my father, it is my honor and privilege to finally put it all down in writing, in vivid detail.

In addition to his almost fatal experiences and eventful upbringing in New York, my father's wartime experiences with Jimmy Stewart are some of the most memorable ones of his entire life, which he was always glad to share. These memories were from the comical to the sublime - from their hilarious first encounter to the dangerous combat missions they flew together in the hellish skies over France and Germany in WWII. To top it off, Stewart personally came to my father's rescue when he was about to be court-martialed as a result of an unfortunate incident. These were subjects he often reflected upon with a grateful attitude, humility, respect, and admiration. My father said that Jimmy Stewart is just like you see him in the movies - a down-to-earth, real guy. The men under his command all admired and respected his skillful leadership, courage, sincere care for the men under his command, and his sterling example. This is a fact my father and his crew, and all the other aircrews, testified to over and over again. This truth is borne in the pages of this book. In it you'll read the incredible stories of my father's extraordinary life and see how the Great Depression molded a generation for combat in World War II. His story is a unique, yet complimentary part of the Greatest Generation's legacy to his family, America, and to our friends 'across the pond' in Europe. They are stories I never grew tired of hearing."

IF A CATS HAVE NINE LIVES, COULD A MAN HAVE THE SAME?

What are the chances that a guy would survive nine separate near-death experiences between early childhood and the age of twenty-two, and not to mention, survive thirty life-threatening combat missions over the war-torn skies of Nazi occupied Europe?

Henry Culver did. He survived...

- a near fatal poisonous infection from a mosquito bite as a five year old in Queens

- a near drowning in the Hell Gate section of the East River in Queens when his home-made raft broke apart

- another near drowning in a strong undertow off of Coney Island

- a mugging, beating, and a fall down a stairwell in junior high school in Brooklyn

- being beaten, and was almost killed, in a gang war in Harlem in upper Manhattan as he was an innocent bystander mistaken for part of a gang

- nearly getting killed when a close burst of flak exploded in front of his ball turret gun position on his plane, and then severe frostbite set in at high altitude during aerial combat over Europe in World War II

- a German anti-aircraft shell's direct hit on his plane while over Nurnberg, Germany, and an emergency landing in England

- a frozen oxygen mask hose and high altitude anoxia while passed out from lack of oxygen on a bombing raid over the German capital of Berlin

- fatal blizzard conditions over New England while on a training flight mission and a resultant emergency landing

- thirty high altitude combat missions at the height of the air war over Europe, while suffering from vertigo and motion-sickness on each mission

From his early childhood through his teen years on the tough streets of New York City, to thirty combat missions over the unfriendly skies of Hitler's Fortress Europe, Hank Culver's experiences are the stories movies are made of. His near-death encounters and city-bred life prepared him for the fight of his life in World War II. Added to that was his unique experience of flying combat missions with a famous motion picture star from that era.

In November of 1942, against his mother's wishes, nineteen year old Henry "Hank" Culver enlisted in the United States Army Air Forces at a time when it was suffering heavy losses in the air war over Europe against the German Air Force. Within a year, this tough, Italian-American, city-bred kid from New York City was on his way to flying some of the most dangerous combat missions with his B-24 Liberator crew in the same European Theater of Operations. Incredibly, Culver's squadron commander, Major Jimmy Stewart, of motion picture fame, flew many of the same perilous raids side by side with Culver's crew during their combat tour.

This is a true life story of a typical kid from an immigrant family in New York who lived an extraordinary resilient life. It is also the unique and complete story of his and his crew's wartime service together with their gallant commander in the deadly skies over northwest Europe during the Second World War.

COMING IN 2018

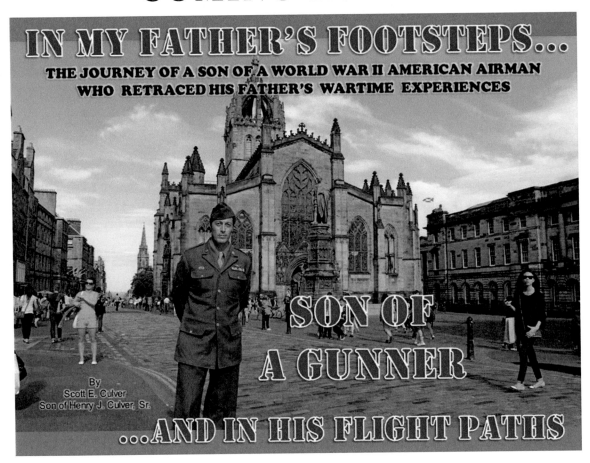

IN MY FATHER'S FOOTSTEPS...
THE JOURNEY OF A SON OF A WORLD WAR II AMERICAN AIRMAN
WHO RETRACED HIS FATHER'S WARTIME EXPERIENCES

By
Scott E. Culver
Son of Henry J. Culver, Sr.

SON OF A GUNNER

...AND IN HIS FLIGHT PATHS

How far, literally and figuratively, would a son go to retrace his father's wartime experiences?

In this photographic journey you will discover how one WWII veteran's son researched and retraced his father's footsteps and flight paths through national and international travel by jet and propeller airplanes... helicopter... rental cars... vans... jeeps... taxis... trucks... buses... trains... monorail... subways... ships... boats... canoe... whitewater rafting... scenic floats... horse and wagon... rickshaws... bicycle... and on foot.

From the author

"Join me in world travel and discovery as I retraced my father's footsteps and flight paths from across the United States to northern Europe in this journey of a lifetime. This photographic essay is filled with hundreds of colorful, vivid photos. In it you'll also see dozens of real WWII photos from my father's and his buddies' collections, as well as famous ones from the war, with many of my color photos placed next to wartime ones, composing 'then and now' shots. It took me five years to cover what my father basically did in three during the war, and there were still more places to travel to!"

"You'll be amazed, like I was, at what my father got to see, visit, and experience in his three years of military service in the Second World War. From the time he was nineteen, until just three weeks before he turned twenty-two years old, he traveled extensively across four different continents. Aside from the war, it was a journey of a lifetime for a young man who never left the New York metro area until he enlisted."

EXTENSIVE TRAVEL ACROSS COUNTRIES AND CONTINENTS

This work is the result of dozens of trips across the U.S. and four tours across Europe by land, air, sea, and rail, as the author covered thousands of miles over a five year period. Hank Culver's son, Scott, posed in similar fashion like his father's wartime photos, in his uniforms and combat gear, at the same places and locations throughout the U.S. and Europe, some 70 years later. Dozens of wartime black and white and color photos, as well as hundreds of current color photos taken by the author during his travels, are included in this volume. This is an amazing journal of the author's five year trek as he retraced his father's wartime footsteps and flight paths from enlistment and stateside training, right on through to his bomber base in England and aerial combat over Europe. It also includes his pilgrimage to the crash site of one of his father's iconic planes, *Nine Yanks and a Jerk,* in Belgium.

UNITED STATES

Stateside towns, cities, and states that his father had been to during WWII included are: Newark, Jersey City, and Atlantic City, New Jersey; Brooklyn, Queens, Manhattan and New York Harbor; Fort Myers, Florida; Goldsboro, North Carolina; Boise and Pocatello, Idaho; Salt Lake City and Wendover, Utah; Sioux City, Iowa; Chicago, Illinois; Lincoln, Nebraska; and West Palm Beach, Florida, just to name a few. His post-combat WWII service role as a gunnery instructor back in Massachusetts are also part of the journal.

EUROPE

Extensive photos were taken at his overseas base at Tibenham Airfield, England, and nearby additional WWII American bomber bases including Seething, Hethel, Old Buckingham, Hardwick, and Thorpe Abbots. Locations and places where his father, his buddies, and Jimmy Stewart also frequented while off duty or on weekend passes and R&R include medieval cities, towns and villages such as: London, Norwich, the village of Tibenham, and Cambridge in England. Scotland stomping grounds include: Prestwick, Edinburgh, and Glasgow. Aerial shots taken over the English Channel and British and French coastlines are also featured. Aerial photographs taken on photo fights over central Scotland and the western Scottish coast near Prestwick are included as well.

Photos portraying his father's trip home on the Queen Mary troopship from Gourock, Scotland to New York City were taken on location, including onboard the Queen Mary. Rare shots of his commanding officer, James "Jimmy" M. Stewart, are included as well, as the author retraced some of his father's commanding officer's footsteps in Ketteringham Hall, England and posed in identical uniforms and similar fashion (in England and in the U.S.) in tribute to the actor turned bomber pilot.

STATESIDE MILITARY BASES AND TRAINING

Stateside military bases, airfields, posts, forts, camps, training areas, regions of note his father flew training over, and sites he had connections with include: Seymour-Johnson Field (now AFB), North Carolina; Buckingham Army Airfield (now airport) in Lehigh Acres and Page Airfield (now airport) in Fort Myers, Florida; Salt Lake City Army Air Base (now airport), Wendover Field, the Bonneville Salt Flats, and Hill Field (now AFB), Utah; Gowen Field (Boise Airport) and Pocatello Army Air Base (now airport), Sun Valley, and Craters of the Moon National Monument in Arco, in Idaho; Jackson Hole, the Grand Tetons and Yellowstone National Parks, Wyoming; Grand Canyon National Park, Arizona; Sioux City Army Air Base (now airport), and Lincoln Army Air Base (now airport), Iowa; Morrison Field (now West Palm Beach airport), and Boca Raton Army Airfield (now airport), Florida; Westover Field (now AFB and airport) and Fort Devens, Massachusetts; Camp Kilmer, Fort Dix, and McGuire AFB, New Jersey. Many pictures were taken from the air from various planes and a helicopter, as well as on the ground.

OVERSEAS MILITARY BASES AND COMBAT

Overseas military bases, airfields, posts, forts, camps, training areas, and regions of note he flew training over, and sites he had connections with include: Boriquen Field, Puerto Rico; Atkinson Field, British Guiana (now Guyana); Parnamirim Field (now Natal AFB) and Val de Caes Field (now Belem airport) in Brazil; Dakar, Senegal; Marrakech, Morocco; RAF Valley, Wales; Tibenham Airfield, England; Prestwick Field (now airport), Scotland;

Normandy, France; Thorembais St. Trond, Belgium. Many aerial shots were taken from private and commercial planes.

Overseas locations related to areas Culver flew combat over, his buddies traveled to, and sites that were key to the Allied victory in WWII are also included, such as: Paris, Versailles, and Normandy in France; Brussels, Bastogne, Ghent, and Bruges in Belgium. One of the author's goals was to record places and sites from World War II in color. Interesting people (famous, foreign, and American) whom the author met and posed with, are also included in the essay.

WWII MUSEUMS AND OTHER PLACES OF INTEREST
Photographs from numerous visits to air museums, train stations, memorials, and historic sites to see WWII planes, tanks, jeeps, trains, ships, equipment, and items for research in the U.S. and in Europe include:

United States
Ohio - The National Museum of the U.S. Air Force in Dayton, and The Champaign Aviation Museum in Urbana; **Washington, D.C.** - The National Archives and Records Administration research center (at College Park), The National Air and Space Museum, The Steven F. Udvar-Hazy Center, The National WWII Memorial, the National Mall and The White House; **Pennsylvania** - The Mid-Atlantic Air Museum in Reading; **Arizona** - The Pima Air and Space Museum and U.S. Air Force 'Boneyard,' in Tucson; **Colorado** - The U.S. Air Force Academy, Peterson AFB and Peterson Air and Space Museum in Colorado Springs; **California** -The Queen Mary cruise ship/troopship in Long Beach, the Planes of Fame and Yanks Air museums in Chino; **Iowa** - The Mid-America Museum of Aviation and Transportation in Sioux City; **Illinois** - Union Train Station in Chicago; **Nebraska** - State Capitol Building in Lincoln; **Louisiana** -The National WWII Museum in New Orleans; **Massachusetts** - The Springfield Armory in Springfield, The Fort Devens Museum in Devens, The Historic Northampton Museum, The World War II Club - The Deuce in Northampton, The Collings Foundation Museum in Stow; **Idaho** - The Idaho Military History Museum, the Idaho State Capitol Building, and the Boise Train Station in Boise, the Pocatello Train Station, Bannock County Historical Museum, and the Idaho State University Library in Pocatello, The Warhawk Air Museum in Nampa, The Legacy of Flight Museum in Rexburg, and Warbirds Cafe in Driggs; **Florida** – The Fantasy of Flight Air Museum in Polk City, Fort Myers Train Station and Southwest Florida Museum of History in Fort Myers; **North Carolina** - Goldsboro Train Station in Goldsboro; **New Jersey** - Central Railroad of New Jersey Terminal, Liberty State Park; **Georgia** - The Mighty Eighth Air Force Museum in Savannah. **Utah** - Union Pacific Train Station, Rio Grande Train Station, and the Utah State Capitol Building in Salt Lake City.

Europe
England – The Royal Palace, Trafalgar Square, Parliament, Charing Cross Train Station, Liverpool Street Train Station, Kings Cross Train Station, Paddington Train Station, and the Imperial War Museum in London, The American Air Museum in Duxford, The Royal Air Force Museum in Hendon, Norwich Train Station, the Norwich Castle and the Norwich Cathedral in Norwich, Seething Control Tower Museum in Seething, The 100th Bomb Group Museum in Thorpe Abbotts, Norfolk and Suffolk Aviation Museum in Flixton, Cambridge Train Station in Cambridge, and The American Cemetery in Maddingly; **Scotland** - Edinburgh and Glasgow Train Stations, The Castle in Edinburgh; **France** - WWII memorials at Port en Bessin, Normandy American Cemetery and Memorial and Omaha Beach in Colleville, Normandy Tank Museum in Catz, Musée du Débarquement and Utah Beach in Sainte-Marie-du-Mont/Utah Beach, Airborne Museum in St. Mere Eglise, Musée Mémorial d'Omaha Beach in Saint-Laurent-sur-Mer, Museum of the Battle of Normandy, the Bayeux Commonwealth War Graves Commission Cemetery in Bayeux, Musée du débarquement and Arromanche 360 in Arromanches, Centre Juno Beach in Courseulles-sur-Mer, Musee du Radar in Douvres-la-Délivrande, German Gun Battery in Longues sur Mer, Pegasus Bridge/Mémorial Pégasus in Ranville, Ranville War Cemetery in Calvados, and The Merville Battery Museum in Merville; **Belgium** - Musee du Souvenir in Maleves, Bastogne Barracks, Bastogne Ardennes 44 Museum, Bastogne War Museum and Memorial, American battle positions in the Hürtgen Forest, German War Cemetery in Bastogne, and Henri-Chapelle American Cemetery and Memorial in Henri-Chapelle.

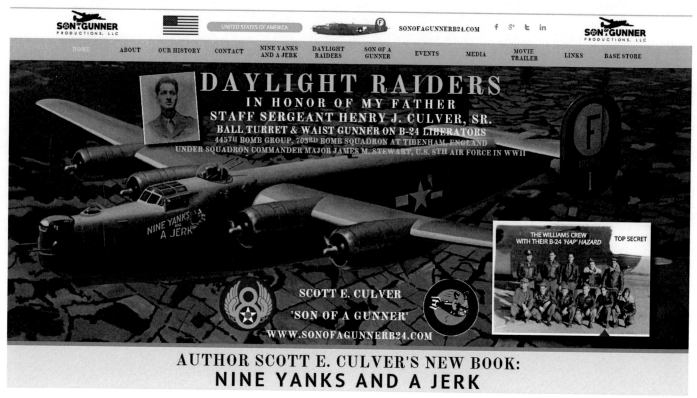

View our colorful Homepage, About, and Our History pages to learn more about who we are. You can also see more details about forthcoming books, events, and media related to all three books and promos – *Nine Yanks and a Jerk*, *Daylight Raiders*, *Son of a Gunner*, and the movie trailer *Daylight Raiders*.

Website features:

Homepage – Discover more info about *Nine Yanks and a Jerk*, reviews for this book, where to purchase additonal copies from, sales and specials, updates.and descriptions about forthcoming books, media links for TV and radio broadcasts, links to news articles, and how to purchase a copy of the vivid print of the plane *Nine Yanks and a Jerk*, called *Daylight Raiders*. Links to other pages are here, including Facebook. **About** – Describes *SonofaGunner Productions*, its mission and goals. **Our History** – Our History details Henry Culver's life story and his son's Scott's life, adventures in travel, research, and writing of his three books. **Contact** - Leave feedback, reviews, comments, and suggestions. **Media** – See Scott's interview on Fox news with Eric Shawn. See the video *Gear Up!* about high altitude bomber gear and combat. Watch Scott narrate and put on his father's heavy bomber gear for high altitude combat as he narrates in front of the Collings Foundation B-24 *Witchcraft*. In addition, there is also a special feature video of his father's last surviving combat buddy, George Snook, telling the story of the mission described in this book. Updates will also be added from Scott's travels across the U.S. and Europe from the last five and a half years as he narrated his father's WWII story across countries and continents. **Events** – Current events from book talks and signings to airshows and reenactments. **Movie Trailer** – Details and teaser trailers from the movie trailer *Daylight Raiders* can be viewed here. **Links** – Search through great websites used in Scott's research, travels and reenactments. **Daylight Raiders** and **Son of a Gunner** - See the overviews and story elements of these two forthcoming books, as well as sample photos from the two volumes.

Made in the USA
Middletown, DE
11 July 2016